Tools for
Teaching
in the Block

This book is dedicated to my husband, Arthur, who supported every page with patience and understanding when dinner was late, the house was a mess, and the laundry piled up while I wrote, revised, and wrote some more. Thanks, Art!

Tools for
Teaching
in the Block

Roberta L. Sejnost

CORWIN
A SAGE Company

For information:

Corwin
A SAGE Company
2455 Teller Road
Thousand Oaks, California 91320
(800) 233-9936
Fax: (800) 417-2466
www.corwinpress.com

SAGE Ltd.
1 Oliver's Yard
55 City Road
London EC1Y 1SP
United Kingdom

SAGE India Pvt. Ltd.
B 1/I 1 Mohan Cooperative Industrial Area
Mathura Road, New Delhi 110 044
India

SAGE Asia-Pacific Pte. Ltd.
33 Pekin Street #02-01
Far East Square
Singapore 048763

Printed in the United States of America.

Library of Congress Cataloging-in-Publication Data

Sejnost, Roberta.
Tools for teaching in the block/Roberta L. Sejnost.
      p. cm.
Includes bibliographical references and index.
ISBN 978-1-4129-5712-0 (cloth)
ISBN 978-1-4129-5713-7 (pbk.)
   1. Block scheduling (Education) 2. High school teaching. 3. Teenagers—Education.
I. Title.

LB3032.2.S49 2009
371.2'42—dc22   2008049671

This book is printed on acid-free paper.

09   10   11   12   13   10   9   8   7   6   5   4   3   2

Acquisitions Editor:	Cathy Hernandez
Editorial Assistant:	Sarah Bartlett
Production Editor:	Cassandra Margaret Seibel
Copy Editor:	Cate Huisman
Typesetter:	C&M Digitals (P) Ltd.
Proofreader:	Susan Schon
Indexer:	Jean Casalegno
Cover Designer:	Michael Dubowe

Contents

Preface

The movement toward the use of "block schedules," with the main goal of increasing the traditional class period of 45–50 minutes to an extended period of up to 90 minutes, has caused apprehension among many middle and high school teachers. Although good reasons are provided for going to a block schedule, some teachers, already concerned about being able to "reach" an increasingly diverse student population, feel unprepared to teach in longer time periods. Teachers wonder: "Students have a hard enough time sitting for 50 minutes; how can I expect them to sit for 90 minutes?" or "I am not sure I can be creative enough for 90 minutes."

Many teachers, committed to reaching all students in their classroom, are searching for ways to best use these new extended periods of time. Rather than merely extending what they had been doing for 50 minutes or simply adding busy work to fill up the time allotments that have been created, teachers want to ensure that they use additional time to actually increase student learning. This book presents research-based best practices and offers a lesson plan format, as well as content area strategies, that enable teachers to increase learning by more effectively integrating reading, writing, and critical thinking into a 90-minute block of instructional time. These strategies are grounded in the theory of multiple intelligences and brain-based research, which can be applied in every classroom, no matter what the subject or grade level. Examples and blackline masters for implementing the strategies are included in this book to assure immediate transfer to all content area classrooms.

Chapter 1 (Preparing to Teach the Adolescent Learner) paints a picture of adolescent learners and their instructional needs. The chapter details methods to best facilitate adolescent learning, including extending the teaching time in the classroom from the usual 45–50 minutes to an extended period of 90 minutes. In order to assure that effective instruction takes place during this extended period of time, the concept of comprehensive curriculum mapping and organized lesson planning is discussed and examples of curriculum maps and 90-minute lesson plans are provided.

Chapter 2 (Tools for Teaching in the Block) presents specific techniques that will most effectively and efficiently help teachers deliver the curriculum and lessons they will teach. Specifically, this chapter provides a discussion and examples of (1) cooperative learning strategies, (2) brain-compatible learning strategies, (3) effective questioning techniques and strategies, and (4) the use of graphic organizers.

Chapter 3 (Entice the Learner) discusses the first phase of the block schedule lesson plan format and provides teachers with strategies to prepare students for learning by fostering recall of their prior knowledge, helping them to set a purpose for reading and learning, teaching them the vocabulary necessary for understanding, and arousing their interest in and motivation for learning.

Chapter 4 (Enlighten the Learner) presents the second phase of the block schedule lesson plan format. In essence, this chapter suggests strategies teachers may use to help students find the information necessary to allow them to proceed to phase three. Specific strategies presented in this chapter are considered in two categories, teacher-centered strategies and teacher-student interactive strategies.

Chapter 5 (Engage the Learner) presents the elements of the third phase of the block schedule lesson plan format. In this chapter, teachers are presented strategies and instructional frameworks—such as study guides, note-taking formats, and graphic organizers—that encourage students to actively interact with and process what they have learned by making predictions, keeping their purpose for reading in mind, self-monitoring their understanding, and making connections between what they are learning (new knowledge) and what they already know (old knowledge). These strategies are presented in two categories: strategies for monitoring learning and strategies for guiding learning.

Chapter 6 (Extend the Learner) presents the final phase of the block schedule time format. During this phase students clarify, reinforce, and extend what they have learned by organizing the information they have gathered and using their critical thinking skills to synthesize, analyze, and evaluate it. In addition, in this phase students have an opportunity to reflect on their learning in order to clarify their understanding, setting them upon the road to lifelong learning. Strategies to accomplish this are the highlight of this chapter.

Chapter 7 (Enact the Learning) provides readers with a summary of the four-phase lesson plan format as well as a listing of the strategies and activities that are appropriate for use in each phase. In addition, a series of lesson ideas for a range of content area disciplines is presented.

Acknowledgments

I wish to thank my colleagues at the Kane County, Illinois, Regional Office of Education and the teachers who teach in Kane County, Illinois, who called my attention to the need to write a book to help teachers effectively teach in a block schedule.

PUBLISHER'S ACKNOWLEDGMENTS

Corwin gratefully acknowledges the contributions of the following reviewers:

Michael A. Baker
Eighth Grade Science
    Teacher/TAG Coordinator
Memorial Middle School
Albany, OR

Jeremy Jones
Assistant Professor of Education
Athens State University College of
    Education
Athens, AL

Eve Lindsay
Seventh Grade Teacher
Monroe Middle School
San Jose, CA

Paul Mack
Associate Professor of Education
Maryville University
St. Louis, MO

Barbara Meyer
Associate Professor
Department of Curriculum and
    Instruction
Illinois State University
Normal, IL

About the Author

 **Roberta L. Sejnost** received her master of education from the University of Illinois at Chicago and her doctorate of education in curriculum and instruction from Loyola University, Chicago. She has been a university professor and is currently literacy consultant to the Regional Office of Education, Kane County, Illinois. She has taught social studies, reading, and English at the secondary school level and courses in literacy, authentic assessment, brain-based learning, multiple intelligences, and cooperative learning at the college level. Sejnost is currently the International Reading Association's state coordinator for Illinois and has been a member of the board of directors for the International Reading Association's Secondary Reading Special Interest Group as well as a member of the executive board of the Illinois Reading Council, and she has served as an officer in several of the Illinois Reading Council's special interest groups.

A nationally recognized staff developer, Roberta is a certified trainer in authentic assessment, brain-based learning, portfolio assessment, multiple intelligences, and reading and writing across content areas. She has presented at more than 200 educational conferences across the country. In addition to authoring this text and coauthoring *Reading and Writing Across Content Areas* (Corwin, 2007), Dr. Sejnost was featured in the videotapes to accompany Drake University's online course EDDL219—Reading Across the Curriculum. In 1986, she was named Teacher of the Year in her district; in 1993, she was awarded the International Reading Association's Contribution to Literacy Award for the State of Illinois; in 1996, she was recognized in *Who's Who of American Educators;* in 2003, she was given the Reading Educator of the Year award for 2003 by the Illinois Reading Council; and in 2007, she was awarded a Certificate of Recognition by the Illinois Reading Council for her contributions to literacy in Illinois.

CHAPTER 1

*P*reparing to Teach the Adolescent Learner

If a child can't learn the way we teach, maybe we should teach the way they learn.

—Ignacio Estrada

THE ADOLESCENT LEARNER: A PROFILE

Today one merely needs to open a newspaper or tune in to a radio or television news broadcast to hear about the so-called crisis in education. Accountability testing, national reform movements, and state report cards have prompted educators and parents to reexamine age-old educational practices in light of the changing nature of our society and the people who populate it. And nowhere has this focus been more strongly applied than in the world of adolescent learning. Adolescents, after all, have the challenge of being "the next generation"; it will be up to them to assure our place in the world through their leadership, initiative, and creativity.

However, to those who currently embrace the task of teaching adolescents, the challenges faced can be daunting. Teaching adolescents is no easy task. Having taught them for some 33 years, I know that, in many respects, the adolescents of today are not that dissimilar to the adolescents of the past. They have boundless energy, their emotional state is always in crisis, and their commitment to learning can vary from day to day, class to class, minute to minute. They tend to live "in the moment," more concerned about what movie to see than about the geometry test on Friday. They strive to be liked and accepted by their peers. Anxious to fit in, they tentatively explore relationships and search to carve out an identity for themselves. They seek to establish control over their lives: They want to be treated as adults, have the freedom to choose, exercise their right to assert an opinion, and make decisions that are respected by others. Yet, even though they embrace these adult-like behaviors, overall they fear failure and making incorrect decisions and choices, and, in some cases, they are uncomfortable with the uncertainty of the future. Yet, all these young adults embrace the hope for a better future for themselves and their families.

However, while the "state" of adolescence has not changed significantly in the last 30 years, the context in which these adolescents live certainly has. Today, the largest generation of adolescents in history, 1.2 billion strong, faces a rapidly changing, fast-paced, technology-driven world where young people derive most of their information about the world, what to expect, and how to behave from their peers and from mass media. Today's adolescents have inherited a world shaped by

- globalization of trade, investment, and economic relationships.
- instantaneous access to information and experiences through mass communications media.
- a changing nature of work, which will require new skills and capacities and may result in the need to change career choices several times, perhaps embracing a choice that does not yet even exist.
- urbanization and migration.
- changing family structures.

In addition to facing the turmoil of a changing society, adolescents themselves are facing great changes. According to information provided in *At the Turning Point: The Young Adolescent Learner* (n.d.), during the adolescent years students undergo a period of significant growth that occurs more rapidly than during any other time in their lives except, of course, during infancy. In effect, they grow physically, emotionally and psychologically, morally and intellectually. Physically, adolescents may sometimes feel restless and tired because they are undergoing huge hormonal changes in their bodies, but at other times they exhibit increased energy and crave physical activity. They are concerned with the changes that are taking place in their bodies, and in their search to develop sexual awareness, they can often be seen touching and bumping into each other. Finally, they are often physically vulnerable, because they are quick to engage in risky behaviors and poor health habits.

Emotional and psychological changes occur as well. They may exhibit mood swings that are intense and unpredictable. They have sudden outbursts of activity because they need to release energy. While they crave independence, acceptance, and an adult identity, they are concerned about their own physical growth and maturity and are self-conscious and sensitive to personal criticism, believing that the problems, feelings, and experiences they face are unique to them *(At the Turning Point,* n.d.*)*.

Morally, adolescents are beginning to grasp an understanding of the issues that face society, and they no longer perceive these issues as "black or white." In their search for this understanding, they rely on adult role models who are trustworthy and will listen to their thoughts and ideas. They rely on these adults for advice but are vehement about making their own decisions. And, while they show an understanding of the difficulty of initiating change, they are often impatient with the time it takes to make that change. In addition, adolescents are quick to judge others but are slow to recognize their own faults *(At the Turning Point,* n.d.*)*.

Finally, the adolescent is changing intellectually. These students have an intense curiosity and are willing to undertake a wide range of intellectual pursuits, although they may fail to sustain many of them over a long period of time. They prefer active, rather than passive, learning experiences shared through interaction with their peers and will exhibit a high level of achievement if they feel challenged and engaged. Finally, as their thinking moves from the concrete to the abstract, they begin to develop the ability to self-reflect *(At the Turning Point,* n.d.*)*.

WHAT CAN TEACHERS DO TO FACILITATE ADOLESCENT LEARNING?

Given what we know about how adolescents grow and change and prepare themselves to exist in a world that is changing as well, educators are faced with the one overriding question: What can we do to facilitate adolescent learning? We are aware that these young people must be able to efficiently maneuver through vast quantities of written and electronic information and communicate effectively orally, verbally, and electronically. They will need to successfully explore, question, analyze, and synthesize information, and they will need to accomplish this all while working collaboratively with their peers. However, to truly facilitate adolescent learning, we must, as Lambert and McCombs (1998) suggest, understand how and under what specific conditions that learning occurs. As good teachers who have successfully taught adolescents over the years and have read the research on best practices, we are aware that in order for adolescents to learn, they must be able to connect what they are learning to what they already know or have personal experience with (Alvermann & Phelps, 2001; Kamil, 2003; Van den Broek & Kremer 2000), and they must be willing and motivated to put forth the effort to learn (Langer, 2001; Moore, Alvermann, & Hinchman, 2000). However, as clarified in the work of Perkins (1992) and Sizer (1996), it is not enough to simply foster students' prior knowledge and get them excited about learning something. Instead, "Adolescent learning involves interactive, purposeful, and meaningful engagement" (Crawford, 2007, p. 5), and happens best, according to Crawford, when adolescents

- encounter developmentally appropriate learning that is presented in multiple ways and in interesting and enjoyable manners.
- are intellectually challenged by authentic tasks that they perceive to be challenging, novel, and relevant to their lives.
- share and discuss ideas and work collaboratively on tasks, projects, and problems.
- utilize multiple strategies to acquire, integrate, and interpret knowledge meaningfully and then demonstrate their understanding and apply their recently found knowledge to new situations.
- are provided opportunities to develop and use strategic thinking skills to reason and problem solve.
- are given guidance and immediate feedback on their progress and encouraged to monitor and reflect upon their personal progress and understanding.
- are situated in a safe, supportive environment where their personal ideas are valued and they are free from fear of punishment and embarrassment. (Crawford, 2007)

A METHOD TO FACILITATE ADOLESCENT LEARNING

The characteristics of today's adolescents and an outline of those conditions that facilitate their learning, as discussed above, have clear implications for the classrooms of today and naturally lead us to the overriding question: What method of instruction will best complement today's adolescents and most effectively help them learn? While a myriad of educational methods and reforms have been suggested across the years, one that has sustained popularity for the past 20 years has been the concept of extending the length of class instruction time from the universally accepted 40- to 60-minute period to class periods of up to 90 to 100 minutes. This movement, Canady and Rettig (1995) suggest, comes from a variety of criticisms of traditional school schedules. These criticisms are centered around the fact that when students are required to pass through six, seven, or eight class periods a day and when teachers are required to teach five or six classes a day,

- instruction is fragmented, so the teacher is not engaged in in-depth teaching, and the student is not engaged in in-depth learning.
- the school takes on an impersonal factory assembly line environment, where teachers are asked to address the intellectual and emotional needs of over 100 or more students, and students are expected to adapt to the differing requirements, standards, and styles of a variety of teachers each day.
- discipline problems increase, because students transition from class to class several times a day, moving through narrow hallways under crowded conditions.
- actual instructional time is limited, so instruction is often accomplished by lecture only rather than the use of comprehensive laboratory work, Socratic seminars, learning centers, or cooperative learning structures.
- the opportunity for extended learning time for students who need it is not provided.

This movement to implement changes in the organization and use of time in middle and high schools comes from a variety of sources. As noted by the 1997 research report, *Alternative High School Schedules: A View From the Teacher's Desk* (Pisapia & Westfall, 1997), the daily schedule a school develops basically drives its curriculum and instructional practices. Yet, the traditional time structure embraced by most middle and high schools has remained essentially the same for a century and is based on the 1910 concept of the Carnegie Unit, which Canady and Rettig (1996) note is determined by seat time rather than the needs of the students, especially those whose learning patterns may differ from those of their peers. However, when the 1983 report *A Nation at Risk* (National Commission on Excellence in Education) reported that students were falling behind their counterparts in other industrialized nations, educators took note and began to consider ways to remedy the problem, toying with the concept of restructuring schools. Queen (2000), in his article "Block Scheduling Revisited," provides a succinct overview of the road that has led to the acceptance of block scheduling as a viable alternative to the traditional time structure used at most middle and high schools. Queen notes that

John Goodlad, in his monumental work, *A Place Called School* (1984), lobbied for creating a daily schedule that embraced larger blocks of instructional time when his study of the traditional school structure revealed it did not meet the needs of learners, since it failed to provide adequate time for individualized instruction, work in laboratories, or experiential situations, remediation, or enrichment. A later study by Canady and Rettig (1995) supported Goodlad's findings, noting that the traditional school day format of seven periods of 45 minutes each allows only 60% of the school day to be devoted to instruction.

Furthermore, as Queen (2000) notes, the trend toward urging that greater blocks of time be devoted to learning continued into the 1990s, and, in 1993, Tom Donahoe posited that any school restructuring effort should include the formal rearrangement of the use of time to foster a more active culture of learning (Donahoe, 1993, in Queen). His suggestion was supported by the National Commission on Time and Learning report *Prisoners of Time* (1994, in Queen) that urged schools to restructure themselves to focus on learning rather than be driven by time constraints. In addition, it suggested the concept of block scheduling, which organized courses of study around extended blocks of time, thus allowing teachers to engage their students in active instruction. This concept was quickly embraced by many, and, according to Queen, this movement to utilize the block-scheduling format in some form has increased from 40% in 1994 to 74% in 1998 and leads to a prediction that within a few years, 75% of all high schools will adopt this format.

While the focus of this book is not to glorify the concept of block scheduling, one cannot ignore the fact that one component of block scheduling revolves around a more effective use of time by extending the class period from 45–50 minutes to 90–100 minutes. And research-based evidence (Bransford, Brown, & Cocking, 2000; Bugaj, 1999) clearly shows the positive influences that extending class time has on teaching and learning. In effect, it provides students with all the conditions detailed by Crawford (2007) as supporting adolescent learning discussed above, and it takes into consideration all the characteristics of adolescent learners detailed earlier in this chapter. Research indicates that teaching students in an extended time period provides adequate time for teachers to

- get to know their students better, since the number of students seen daily and the number of classes taught daily is reduced.
- introduce and reinforce concepts to be learned in a single class period.
- utilize cooperative learning strategies.
- allow students to effectively utilize technology.
- make accommodations for individual learning styles.

- promote student inquiry as a method for achieving greater understanding.
- provide more hands-on activities for students.
- conduct laboratory classes that focus on in-depth learning experiences.

And, according to Canady and Rettig (1996), adolescents also benefit because

- the number of classes students must attend and prepare for is reduced.
- students are provided variable amounts of time to learn if they need it.
- students have more opportunities for accelerated learning.
- student learning and teacher instruction time is not fragmented, thus allowing for extensive practice, active learning strategies, and greater student involvement.

Unfortunately, while the positive effects of teaching in an extended time period are clear, the concept itself has caused some apprehension among middle and secondary schools teachers as they struggle with how to keep their students actively engaged in learning for 90–100 minutes. Merely lecturing while students take notes and then having them engage in busy work or begin their homework to fill the time just won't work with today's adolescents, who are used to the fast paced world of technological gadgets and tools. Thus, teachers committed to reaching all students need strategies and activities that will help students make effective use of these new extended periods of class time while increasing their learning. It is the purpose of this text to provide such strategies and activities.

THE FIRST STEPS: CURRICULUM MAPPING AND LESSON PLANNING

However, before teachers can begin to make effective use of the extended periods of class time made available to them, they must consider two over-riding elements: curriculum and lesson planning. To do this effectively, teachers must answer the following questions:

1. What content and skills will be taught? (The Curriculum)
2. How will this content and these skills be taught? (The Lesson Plan)
3. How will this content be assessed? (The Lesson Plan)

Furthermore, in this age of accountability, it is especially crucial that administrators, teachers, parents, and students clearly understand what is being taught and, more important, what students are really learning. The following sections of this text will address these issues in detail.

Curriculum Mapping

The concept of the curriculum is crucial to the success of teaching in an extended time period because, as Canady and Rettig (1996) note, "It is both wise and necessary to create a curriculum pacing guide" (p. 21), because it forestalls teachers from either simply stacking two single class periods upon each other or falling prey to the idea that they have lots of time to teach the curriculum and then running out of that time as the year draws to a close. In fact, according to Hayes-Jacobs as found in Merenbloom and Kalina (2007), mapping the curriculum not only identifies the essential learnings students need but also aligns with the curriculum the content and skills students will need to learn. In addition, the identification of these essential learnings lays the path for a rigorous curriculum and becomes the focus for both the formative and summative assessments given to evaluate those essential learnings (National Association of Secondary School Principals, 2006). As noted by Jacobs (1997), "If a commitment does not exist for when something will be taught, it will not be taught" (p. 4).

The concept of curriculum mapping can be traced back to the work of Dr. Heidi Hayes Jacobs (1997) and is, in reality, a process used to develop a database of the curriculum of a school. It presents a way to document how the various components of the curriculum relate to one another. If used effectively, curriculum mapping can become an analytic communication and planning tool. In other words, it is a method for identifying, collecting, and recording the core skills and content taught, the processes used to teach the skills and content, and the assessment used to determine whether students have learned the content. In effect, it is a true representation of what is really being taught, tested, and learned in the classroom.

While most school have complex curriculum guides that trace what students should know and be able to do, few actually focus in on what specific content and skills are used in instruction, the time frame students follow as they learn this content and these skills, and what assessments teachers use to determine whether students have learned what they have been taught. In essence, curriculum maps may be used for

- providing communication among teachers.
- aligning instruction to standards and outcomes.
- developing a framework for building instructional units.
- facilitating grade level planning.
- developing integrated or cross-curricular curriculums.

- providing a baseline for the curriculum review and renewal process and identifying unnecessary redundancies, inconsistencies, misalignment, weaknesses, and gaps in the curriculum.
- identifying staff development needs.

Coupled with traditional curriculum guides, the process of curriculum mapping "amplifies the possibilities for long-range planning, short-term preparation and clear communication" (Jacobs, 1997, p. 5), thus not only enhancing the learning of the students but fostering a climate of effective collaboration with a school.

The Process of Curriculum Mapping

The journey a school takes as it creates its curriculum map may be a variegated one, since schools have a plethora of components to choose from in creating the map as well as a variety of methods to follow as they work through the mapping process. As a result, one school's curriculum map may well differ from another's, as each will reflect those components that best help the school to gain insight into what students are truly experiencing and learning. As Jacobs (2004) notes, "Curriculum maps have the potential to become the hub for making decisions about teaching and learning," and thus, "Mapping becomes an integrating force to address not only curriculum issues, but also programmatic ones" (p. 126).

While curriculum mapping is most effective when undertaken by an entire school staff, much success has also been seen in schools where the task is first attempted by one or two teachers mapping one or two classes or courses and then allowed to grow and blossom as other teachers see the enormous benefits of completing the process and turn their energies to the mapping process. In addition, while a myriad of software programs exists to facilitate the construction of curriculum maps, such as (1) Atlas Curriculum Management System (http://www.rubiconatlas.com/mapping.htm), (2) Curriculum Creator (http://www.ael.org), (3) Curriculum Mapper (http://www.clihome.com/curriculummapper), (4) MapSter (http://mapster.gstboces.org), (5) Perspective Curriculum Map (fmdonaldson@earthlink.com), (6) Quality Leadership by Design (http://www.qld-llc.com), and (7) TECHPATHS (Info@perfpathways.com), the use of a computer-based program is not essential, since many schools have completed the mapping process using a simple curriculum map template developed using a basic word-processing program. A blackline master of such a template is included in Figure 1.6 at the end of this chapter.

Once teachers have decided to undertake the process of curriculum mapping, they need to choose the components that will drive their mapping task. As noted above, there are several components that can be included within the map. Among the most common are (1) the essential question, (2) time frame, (3) content, (4) skills, (5) assessments, and (6) resources. Each of these will be discussed below.

Essential Questions

Essential questions are complex questions that serve as the basis of the instructional units and guide student learning. By centering on major issues, problems, or themes, they help keep the curriculum focused. Effective essential questions are open-ended and of a high order, so they provoke deep thought and critical thinking rather than mere retention of facts. Finally, an important aspect of creating an essential question is that it must emphasize the why and how of the topic rather than the what. Jacobs (1997) suggests that the following criteria for writing essential questions be followed: Questions should

1. be phrased so that students can easily understand them.
2. be written in broad, organizational terms.
3. be reflective of the concepts that students will study in the curriculum.
4. be distinct and substantial.
5. avoid repetition.
6. be realistically addressed within the time frame allotted to their study.
7. be logical in sequence.
8. be posted in classrooms for all students to see.

Time Frame

While this component seems like it would be the easiest to develop, it is often the one that is most quickly revised or changed. In essence, the mapping of the time devoted to each content topic can be accomplished in a variety of ways. Some teachers utilize "diary mapping," developing a year-long log of what they have actually taught, while others develop a "consensus map," which presents a sort of bottom line of what all students must learn and be able to do. An easy way to generate the initial map is to develop a basic calendar using the Calendar Wizard function in Microsoft Word. Once the calendar has been created, teachers should enter all information that reflects a change in the usual school day process, such as days classes do not meet, early release or late start days, and days when assemblies are held as well as when grading periods begin and end. After these items have been entered, teachers may then record the number of days to be devoted to each aspect of the content to be covered. See Figure 1.1 for an example of a curriculum calendar.

Example of Curriculum Calendar
Curriculum Calendar for: <u>Science, Grade: 7</u>

September

Sun	Mon	Tue	Wed	Thu	Fri	Sat
						1
2	3 Labor Day No School	4 District Workshop	5 District Workshop	6 Class Introduction; Housekeeping	7 Class Introduction; Housekeeping	8
9	10 Science Safety Rules	11 Scientific Method	12 Scientific Method	13 Scientific Method	14 Scientific Method	15
16	17 Units of Measurement	18 Units of Measurement	19 Units of Measurement	20 Units of Measurement	21 Units of Measurement	22
23	24 Structure of Life: Animal Cells	25 Structure of Life: Animal Cells	26 Structure of Life: Animal Cells	27 Structure of Life: Animal Cells	28 Plant Cells	29
30						

2007

Figure 1.1

Content

When completing the content portion of the curriculum map, teachers need to recognize that they are not developing a lesson plan for the content to be covered but, rather, are merely listing the major concepts within the content that will be covered. Content is best defined as the subject matter or the key concepts, facts, and events of a discipline, and it is usually organized around topics, issues, works of literature, art or music, a problem, or themes. Examples of content are (1) multiplication or fractions in mathematics classes, (2) narrative writing or *Othello* in English classes, (3) revolutions or the death penalty in social studies classes, and (4) water pollution or electricity in science classes. Note: The content to be studied is expressed as a noun.

Skills

Once the content to be learned has been identified, the teacher must clearly identify what precise skills need to be taught, learned, or used in order for students to successfully master the content. Basically, two types of skills exist: precision skills that are related to specific disciplines like math, science, and English and that identify what students must be able to do in order to learn in a specific content; and cross-disciplinary skills that are used in all disciplines, such as reading, listening, speaking, editing, and revising. Examples of skills are (1) classify plants based on structure in science classes; (2) convert mixed numbers to improper fractions in mathematics classes; and (3) locate, access, and use maps, charts, and graphs in social studies. Often the list of key skills in a discipline is a great deal longer than the list of content items identified, because each skill must be specifically described. Note: the skills students exhibit are expressed as verbs.

Assessment

Assessments are best defined as the observable evidence, whether it be a product or a performance, that learning has occurred. In effect, assessments are designed to reveal how students have acquired the skills and learned the content studied. This component of the curriculum is crucial, because it identifies how the teacher will know if the students have learned what has been taught. Therefore, the assessments listed should be both formative and summative as well as formal and informal. In addition, assessment strategies for both skills and content should be identified, and the forms the assessments take should be reflective of the learning outcomes desired.

Resources

A final component of the curriculum map is a list of resources, which may include texts, novels, CD-ROMs, films, Web sites, et cetera.

Figure 1.2 provides a curriculum map for social studies, and Figure 1.3 provides an example of a curriculum map for English/language arts. Figure 1.5 at the end of this chapter presents a blackline master for the curriculum map template.

As noted earlier, making the transition from teaching in a traditional time format to teaching in an extended time period requires that we pay attention not only to the question of curriculum, or what content and skills will be taught, but also to the question of how this content and these skills will be taught and how they will be assessed. While mapping answers the question of curriculum, the question of how the curriculum will be taught and assessed is better addressed through the use of effective lesson plan formats.

Example of Curriculum Map for Social Studies

Curriculum Map for Unit on the Road to the Civil War

Time	Essential Questions	Content	Skills	Standards	Assessments	Suggested Activities	Materials/Resources
3 weeks	What political, social, and economic factors caused the Civil War? What were the conflicting perspectives on slavery? What is to be done with the institution of slavery? Must sectionalism ultimately lead to disunion?	Road to the Civil War	Explain causes of the Civil War. Discuss importance of slavery, states' rights, sectionalism. Compare and contrast Union and Confederate states.	**16.A.3b** Make inferences about historical events and eras using historical maps and other historical sources. **16.D.3** (W) Identify the origins and analyze consequences of events that have shaped world social history including famines, migrations, plagues, slave trading.	Civil War Portfolio: compare/contrast North and South Analysis of political cartoon Graph data of Civil War Flow chart of Civil War progress Unit Test Debate over secession/slavery Civil War newspaper	T-charts to compare/contrast strengths, weaknesses, objectives of North and South PowerPoint presentations highlighting key events of war Graph of Civil War data comparing North and South on a variety of measures Map of major battle sites, defining the Union and Confederate states, position of Union blockade, and major troop movements Chart showing battles, objectives, outcomes to accompany map Reading of primary source documents Reading and discussion of significance of Emancipation Proclamation, Gettysburg Address, Lee's surrender, and results of the war	*The American Journey,* Glencoe. Chapter 16 *American History: The Early Years,* Glencoe. Chapter 18 *American Nation,* Prentice Hall. Chapter 17 *Creating America,* McDougall Littell. Chapters 16, 17 *Ordinary Americans: U.S. History Through the Eyes of Everyday People,* Linda R. Monk, Close-Up Publications. Primary source document. Civil War photographs. Activities in *History Alive,* Sections 2 and 3 Web organizers Battle charts Civil War time line

Figure 1.2

Example of Curriculum Map for English/Language Arts

Curriculum Map for Unit on *The Grapes of Wrath*

Time	Essential Questions	Content	Skills	Standards	Assessments	Suggested Activities	Materials/Resources
3 weeks	How did the Great Depression affect the common man? What great changes came about in the United States as a result of the Great Depression? What lessons for the future did the Great Depression teach us?	*The Grapes of Wrath* Analytical reading Figurative language Literary elements Author's style	Respond to passages. Analyze appropriate selections from appropriate sources. Identify purpose of specific setting. Identify and paraphrase dialect and idiomatic language. Identify author's purpose with point of view. Identify historical relevance of novels. Compare and contrast the pursuits of characters in novels with the social attitudes of the 1920s and 1930s.	1.8.17 Identify the outcome or conclusion of a story or nonfiction account based on previous occurrences or events. 1.8.18 Identify the causes of events in a story or nonfiction account. 1.8.19 Draw inferences, conclusions, or generalizations about text and support them with textual evidence and prior knowledge. 2.8.03 Identify the author's message or theme.	Open-response questions Formal essay Formal exam	Read *The Grapes of Wrath*. Read positive and negative reviews of novel. Analyze lyrics of "The Ghost of Tom Joad" by Bruce Springsteen. Examine Dorothea Lange's photography and relate to the Great Depression and *The Grapes of Wrath*. Read "The American Dream." Discussion: Socratic seminar/shared inquiry Reciprocal teaching Reflective journal	*Reader's Handbook* Question-Answer Relationship strategy Film clips: *The Grapes of Wrath* Lyrics: "The Ghost of Tom Joad," Bruce Springsteen Newspaper articles—downward mobility

Figure 1.3

Lesson Plan Formats

Lesson plans serve as guides to help teachers select the best time frame, activities, and assessments to use to help students understand the concepts they are being taught. Williams and Dunn (2008), in their text *Brain Compatible Learning for the Block,* liken good lesson plans unto recipes, blueprints, and game plans that engage students in a successful learning process. While there are a myriad of possibilities for lesson plan formats, almost all of them suggest that students move through at least three transitions during the extended class period. Canady and Rettig (1996) propose the following three parts and the time frames for each:

- Explanation: A 25- to 30-minute block of time devoted to presenting information to students through mini-lectures, reviews, modeling, demonstrations, viewing video clips, or textual reading

- Application: A 40- to 60-minute block of time when students are engaged in active learning strategies

- Synthesis: A 15- to 30-minute block of time when students reflect on and are evaluated on what they have learned

In addition, they offer that the three stages described above may be broken down into the lesson format illustrated in Figure 1.4.

Lesson Plan Format

Phase	Elements of Phase	Time Frame
Presentation	Homework review	10–15 minutes
	Presentation	20–25 minutes
Application	Activity	30–35 minutes
	Guided practice	10–15 minutes
Synthesis	Reteach	10–15 minutes
	Closure	5–10 minutes

Figure 1.4

Williams and Dunn (2008) provide yet another lesson plan format that is based the concept of the "three-story" intellect championed in the work of Bellanca and Fogarty (2003) and follows what Williams and Dunn identify as the natural progression of the learning process, wherein the learner

- identifies past experiences and their impact on the learner's knowledge and perception of the topic to be studied.
- is provided opportunities to gain new insights, information, and understandings and to make appropriate connections.
- is encouraged to act on the information and participate in complex tasks.
- is encouraged to apply the concepts, skills, and information in new settings.

The stages of this lesson plan format are (1) the *Inquire Phase,* (2) the *Gather Phase,* (3) the *Process Phase,* and (4) the *Apply Phase.*

As noted above, Williams and Dunn's (2008) lesson plan format follows the natural progression of learning and, as such, also mimics the stages of the reading process: before reading, during reading, and after reading, a format that has been proved effective for learning across all curricular disciplines. The reading process, first observed by Robinson in 1978, centers on providing activities for students to do before their eyes meet the page, while their eyes are on the page, and after their eyes have left the page, since during the stages of this process students construct their own knowledge, which is different from merely acquiring information. In effect, during the process, students activate prior knowledge, monitor and repair their comprehension, make inferences, draw conclusions, set purposes for their learning, and formulate the questions that will serve to guide their learning. Finally, they utilize what they have learned by applying it to new, creative, real-life situations.

Both Canady and Rettig (1996) and Williams and Dunn (2008) provide a strong format for what a good lesson in an extended time period might look like. Furthermore, according to Merenbloom and Kalina (2007), "The foundation for student success rests on a series of carefully constructed activities, scaffolds, or learning engagements that lead to formative or summative assessment" (p. 144). And Sousa (2006) stresses that, in order to maximize learning during a class period, teachers need to give credence to the adolescent brain's need for novelty and quick-paced action and to orchestrate a series of short activities that last approximately 20 minutes each and vary in type to ensure more prime-time learning and less down time. This is further supported by Merenbloom and Kalina, who remind us that the brain cannot remain intensely focused for long periods of time, so effective learning and better retention occur when lessons are divided into 10- to 20-minute segments. Such short learning experiences, according to Sousa, heighten students' retention, fortify their ability to make connections, and thus lead to a better understanding of what they have been taught.

In addition, armed with this information and the theoretical underpinnings of the lesson formats of both Canady and Rettig (1996) and Williams and Dunn (2008) discussed above, I have created the following lesson format that will serve as the basis for the instructional strategies presented in this text. The format has four phases, each varying in time from 10 to 25 minutes. These phases are

1. Phase 1: Entice the Learner, approximately 10–15 minutes in length
2. Phase 2: Enlighten the Learner, approximately 15–20 minutes in length
3. Phase 3: Engage the Learner, approximately 20–30 minutes in length
4. Phase 4: Extend the Learner, approximately 20–25 minutes in length

Each phase of this lesson plan format will be discussed in detail in Chapters 3, 4, 5, and 6 of this text, and appropriate instructional strategies to use during each phase will be presented. It is important to note, however, that while the strategies suggested for each phase can easily be utilized in both traditional class periods and extended class periods, their real power lies in the fact that, when the strategies are utilized in an extended time frame, students are allocated additional time to complete the strategies in depth and with greater understanding. Furthermore, in an extended time frame or block schedule, as students engage in the strategies, they can smoothly transition through each phase of the learning process, sometimes spiraling back upon one phase or another as needed, thereby not only intensifying the learning experience for them but assuring that their learning is successful. An overview of what such lessons might look like can be seen in Chapter 7. Finally, Figure 1.6 at the end of this chapter provides a blackline master for the one-day lesson plan format, and Figure 1.7 presents a blackline master for the week-long template for content areas, while Figure 1.8 provides a template for English/language arts classes.

CHAPTER SUMMARY

Teaching adolescents today can be a challenge. However, current research into what constitutes best practices in teaching and learning provides a myriad of excellent methods that, if utilized, can help facilitate adolescent learning. One of these methods is extending the teaching time in the classroom from the usual 45–50 minutes to an extended period of 90 minutes, often referred to as the block schedule format. However, in order to facilitate learning in the block schedule, best practice suggests the development of a comprehensive curriculum map that details the scope and sequence of the content and skills students are taught and the assessments that illustrate that the content and skills have been learned. Finally, in an effort to effectively meet the needs of the adolescent student enrolled in the block schedule, best practice dictates that teachers utilize an organized lesson plan format that carefully and concisely moves students through the 90 minute class period while keeping them successfully enticed, engaged, enlightened, and extended, thus motivating them to learn. This chapter has focused on these three elements and has provided a plan of action to help guide the reader along a path to accomplish them. The next chapter will feature a series of tools that have proved to be successful in delivering instruction in an extended block schedule class period format.

BLACKLINE MASTERS

Blackline masters for implementing the strategies in this chapter may be found on pages 19 through 22.

Curriculum Map for _____

Time	Essential Questions	Content	Skills	Standard(s)	Assessments	Suggested Activities	Materials/Resources

Figure 1.5

One-Day Lesson Plan Template

Consult the standards and list those that can be addressed in the unit.

As you plan your lesson, consider what teaching and learning experiences will equip students to demonstrate the targeted understandings?

What will students need to know or understand as a result of this lesson?
What will students be able to do as a result of this lesson?
What assessments will show what students know and are able to do?

Topic:

Step	Time	Strategies	Assessment
Excite the Learner	Suggested time: 10–15 minutes		
Objectives	Suggested time: 3–5 minutes		
Enlighten the Learner	Suggested time: 15–20 minutes		
Engage the Learner	Suggested time: 20–30 minutes		
Extend the Learner	Suggested time: 20–25 minutes		

Figure 1.6

Weekly Lesson Plan Template

Part I. Identify desired results: What essential questions and concepts will focus this unit? What will students understand as a result of this unit?

Part II. Plan learning experiences and instruction: Given the targeted understandings, other unit goals, and the assessment evidence identified, what knowledge and skills are needed?

Part III. Consult the standards, and list those that can be addressed in the unit.

Students will need to know:

Students will need to be able to do:

Assessment: To show what students know and are able to do, students will:

		Monday	Tuesday	Wednesday	Thursday	Friday
Excite the Learner	Strategies:					
	Assessment:					
Objectives						
Enlighten the Learner	Strategies:					
	Assessment:					
Engage the Learner	Strategies:					
	Assessment:					
Extend the Learner	Strategies:					
	Assessment:					

Figure 1.7

21

Language Arts/Literature Lesson Plan Template

Desired results of unit: Students will apply inference strategy when reading, practice narrative writing, increase vocabulary.

Knowledge and skills needed: Students will need to know how to communicate, listen, read independently, and write.

State standards: 1. Read with understanding. 2. Read literature from different perspectives. 3. Write for a variety of purposes. 4. Listen and speak effectively for different purposes.

	Monday	Tuesday	Wednesday	Thursday	Friday
Entice the Learner Warm-up:10 minutes					
Enlighten the Learner Read/think aloud 20 minutes					
Enlighten the Learner Shared Reading 20 minutes					
Engage the Learner Guided reading groups 20 minutes					
Engage the Learner Independent reading 20 minutes					
Engage the Learner Word work/vocabulary 20 minutes					
Engage the Learner Spelling 15 minutes					
Enlighten the Learner Writing mini lesson 15 minutes					
Extend the Learner Shared, guided, or independent writing: 20 minutes					

Figure 1.8

Source: Developed by Cynthia Bolanowski, Kane County Regional Office of Education, Geneva, Illinois.

CHAPTER 2

Tools for Teaching in the Block

More important than the curriculum is the question of the methods of teaching and the spirit in which teaching is given.

—Bertrand Russell

WHAT ARE THE TOOLS?

While establishing a solid curriculum through curriculum mapping and developing solid instruction through well-thought-out lesson plans are excellent places to begin the journey of teaching in a block schedule, every teacher knows that there are also tools that must be employed in order to deliver the curriculum effectively. Merenbloom and Kalina (2007) and Wolfe (2001) both stress that the most powerful strategies teachers can use are those that will increase their students' retention, understanding, and application of the content they have learned. Furthermore, according to Williams and Dunn (2008), "When the classroom is a complex, dynamic environment, students can engage in activities that demand several brain and thought processes simultaneously. When this occurs, energy rises, motivation intensifies, and learning increases" (p. 31). And, they note, such a classroom is a brain-compatible classroom, a classroom that is student-centered rather than teacher-centered, where the teacher utilizes multiple approaches such as cooperative learning, multiple intelligence theory, higher order questioning, and graphic organizers to teach the students, and where students have choices in how they learn and how to show that learning. Such a classroom, they state, fully involves students in their learning and helps them advance the concepts they are learning from their short-term working memory system to their long-term memory system.

WHAT CONSTITUTES A BRAIN-COMPATIBLE CLASSROOM?

Today we know more about the brain than in any other time in the past. For example, we now know that the brain weighs about three pounds, is the size of a small grapefruit, and contains over 100 billion neurons, or nerve cells. Messages that we receive through what we see, hear, smell, taste, and touch travel along the 30,000 miles of neuron connections in the cerebral cortex at speeds from 100 to 250 miles per hour, sending information. All this knowledge has made educators and parents alike wonder exactly how the brain thinks and learns and what classroom conditions facilitate this thinking and learning. Fogarty (2001) notes that brain-compatible classrooms are brain-friendly places where "the teaching/learning process is dictated by how the brain functions and how the mind learns" (p. 71). Such classrooms, she notes, are safe, stimuli-rich environments where a balance between direct instruction and authentic learning engage all students in challenging experiences that are designed to respect their individual intelligences, learning styles, and interests and to allow time for them to self-monitor and self-reflect on what they are learning.

In addition, Williams and Dunn (2008) remind us that a brain-compatible classroom depends upon a brain-compatible teacher and provides nine facets of brain-compatible learning that must be addressed as teachers provide an enriched learning experience for their students by focusing on the learner, the content, and the activity. Interestingly enough, these nine facets embrace many of the 12 principles of the brain-compatible classroom espoused by Geoffrey and Renate Caine (2008). The nine facets and the elements of the learning experience that they foster as described by Williams and Dunn are discussed below. Facets 1, 2, and 3 address the learner; Facets 4, 5, and 6 address the content; and Facets 7, 8, and 9 address the activity.

Facet 1: **Learning becomes relevant through personal context.** Williams and Dunn (2008) note that when students connect what they are learning to material they perceive as useful to them in real life, the brain becomes more alert and focused on the learning task. This dovetails with Caine and Caine's (2008) principle that in the human being the search for meaning is innate and that students will learn much more efficiently when their ideas, interests, and purposes are honored. Thus, brain-compatible teachers must strive to make sure that their students clearly see the connections between what they are learning and their lives.

Facet 2: **Learning is dependent upon motivation.** Much of what we know about the physiology of the brain tells us that the limbic system, or the emotional brain, plays a huge part in what we will learn and remember, because, as Caine and Caine (2008) remind us, emotions are involved every time we think, make a decision, or give a response. It is a great part of how we understand or make sense of things. Thus, Williams and Dunn (2008) stress that brain-compatible teachers must understand what motivates their students and incorporate motivational strategies in their teaching.

Facet 3: **Learning is reinforced through hands-on experience.** As Caine and Caine (2008) note, all learning engages one's physiology, and students comprehend more efficiently when they are engaged in experiences that require them to use both their senses and their bodies. This correlates to the concept of the hands-on experience that Williams and Dunn (2008) describe, since, as they note, hands-on activities incorporate practical, physical, and metacognitive skills while asking students to dissect concepts, skills, and information into their individual parts, examine them, and then weave them all back together, thus placing their learning into a context that they can easily understand.

Facet 4: **Learning requires linking new information to prior knowledge.** Caine and Caine (2008) remind us that the brain's search for meaning involves the ability to perceive and create patterns and then link those newly created patterns to patterns that already exist. It is this concept linking the old to the new that is synonymous with the concept of connecting to one's prior knowledge. Furthermore, Fisher and Frey (2008) tell us that the first step to initiating the learning process is activating students' prior knowledge, and Vacca and Vacca (2008) agree and stress that the two most appropriate questions that students can ask are, "What do I need to know?" and "How well do I already know it?" In addition, Williams and Dunn (2008) tell us that we need to help students make connections between what they are to learn and the knowledge they already possess, because the brain is limited in its ability to process unrelated facts but has an unlimited ability to process information it can connect and relate to what it already knows.

Facet 5: **Learning is achieved more efficiently when information is "chunked."** Gopnik, Meltzoff, and Kuhl (1999) remind us that, as adults, we know that we all want things to make sense, and they call this the "explanatory drive." Furthermore, Caine and Caine (2008) tell us that the brain is capable of processing both parts, or individual details, and whole concepts. Thus, making sense of what is to be learned requires that students pay attention to both a big picture and the individual parts. In addition, as discussed above, Caine and Caine (2008) stress that the brain is a pattern seeker, organizing and categorizing information into pattern and matching the information to an already established pattern, or creating a new pattern. Thus, realizing that the brain can process different kinds of information simultaneously, and since the brain is inclined to search for patterns, Williams and Dunn (2008) suggest that if teachers chunk information for their students, the brain will be more able to create a schema, or a pattern, in order to understand the information.

Facet 6: **Learning is enhanced with time for reflection.** Caine and Caine (2008) tell us that learning is both conscious and unconscious and that students will process what they have learned more effectively when provided with time to reflect on their learning. In effect, it is during the reflection process that students can take time to organize, synthesize, analyze, and evaluate what they have learned so they can easily understand, retrieve, and act upon it. Richardson and Morgan (2003) note that it is this reflection on learning that helps students clarify their thinking and focus their understanding so they can better retain what they have learned, because the more one reflects on what has been read and learned, the longer it will be remembered and the more likely it will be used. Furthermore, they posit, additional by-products of this reflection phase are that students become critical thinkers and autonomous or independent learners.

Facet 7: **Learning is retained longer when associated with senses and emotions.** As noted in the discussion regarding Facet 2, much of what we know about the physiology of the brain tells us that the limbic system, or the emotional brain, plays a huge part in what we will learn and remember. It is that part of the brain that governs our likes, dislikes, biases, and prejudices and is involved in almost every thought and decision we make. Caine and Caine (2008) recognize this in their fifth principle that states that since emotions are critical to patterning and ease of learning, students should elicit emotion before, during, and after learning. In addition, Sylwester (1995) informs us that emotions elicit paying attention, and Fisher and Frey (2008) suggest that if students do not pay attention, they will not be able to process the information they are given. In sum, Williams and Dunn (2008) stress that emotions are vital to the storage and recall of information.

Facet 8: **Learning occurs for the greatest number in an environment that fosters and accommodates various ways of being smart.** As early as 1983, Harvard psychologist Howard Gardner identified his theory of multiple intelligences, or ways of being smart, and described seven intelligences. In 1995, he identified an eighth intelligence and is now considering the addition of a ninth, the existential intelligence. According to Gardner, every person possesses all nine of these intelligences at some level, and most people can develop each intelligence to an acceptable level of competency if that intelligence is awakened and amplified and taught. Caine and Caine (2008) further support this facet with their twelfth principle that clarifies that each brain is uniquely organized, which gives credence to the fact that students will learn better when they engage their individual talents, abilities, and capacities. Thus, Williams and Dunn (2008) emphasize that teachers must face the challenge of recognizing and developing and enhancing the intelligence gifts of their students.

Facet 9: **Learning is a high-energy activity.** Brain research tells us that new information disappears within a very short time due to the limited power of short-term memory. Thus, Williams and Dunn (2008) stress that, unless teachers revisit and reinforce the new information taught in a variety of ways, it will disappear. They suggest that a period of intense learning be followed by a period of low-impact reflection.

Given the above facets developed by Williams and Dunn (2008) and entwined with the 12 principles of brain-based learning espoused by Caine and Caine, our thoughts turn to what instructional strategies are best utilized when teaching in an extended time period. Canady and Rettig (1996), early advocates of the block scheduling format, Fogarty (2001), and Williams and Dunn (2008) suggest the following:

- cooperative learning
- use of multiple intelligence theory
- effective questioning techniques
- graphic organizers

All of these strategies are effective when used in an extended time period and are considered brain-compatible, since they fully engage students in learning, thus advancing information students have learned from their short-term memory into their long-term memory (Williams and Dunn, 2008). Each of these techniques will be discussed in detail below.

THE HISTORY OF COOPERATIVE LEARNING

Cooperative learning has a long history. According to Bellanca and Fogarty (2003), the first semblance of cooperative learning came during the emergence of the modern factory system, where educational leaders of the time such as Parker, Dewey, Washington, and Deutsch advocated the model, and, in 1889, Pepitone, Twiner, and Triplet began to formally experiment with cooperative learning in the classroom. However, as Bellanca and Fogarty (2003) note, it was the work of Johnson and Johnson and Slavin that brought the true power of the cooperative learning technique to light. This power of cooperative learning was further clarified by the meta-analysis of Joyce, Weil, and Calhoun (2003), who validated that when cooperative learning is used, students of all ages and in all content areas show improvement in self-esteem, social skills, and academic learning goals. Furthermore, in over 600 studies conducted by Johnson and Johnson (1979, 1999), it was found that the use of cooperative learning leads to

- higher academic performance.
- increased critical thinking skills.
- improved short- and long-term memory abilities.
- better self-esteem.
- positive interaction between and among students.
- increased intrinsic motivation.
- increased emotional involvement in the learning process.

In addition, the findings of the 2000 National Reading Panel's comprehensive review of research on comprehension of text established cooperative learning to be a scientifically sound comprehension tool. Finally, Vacca and Vacca (2008) noted that "within the learning environment created by cooperative groups, students produce more ideas, participate more, and take greater intellectual risks. A cooperative group, with its limited audience, provides more opportunity for students to contribute ideas to a discussion and take chances in the process" (p. 366).

The Framework for Cooperative Learning

In order to effectively employ cooperative learning in the classroom, teachers need to be aware of the principles established by its creators. While several theorists and practitioners such as Johnson and Johnson, Kagan, and Slavin have contributed to the development of cooperative learning by creating their own models, all suggest a certain framework that needs to be incorporated in any cooperative learning model utilized in a classroom. These principles are best set forth by Johnson, Johnson, and Holubec (1993) and posit that in cooperative learning groups, students will engage in

- face-to-face interaction by engaging in small, heterogeneous groups as they support each other in their learning.
- individual accountability by accepting responsibility for successfully engaging in the group's activities and successfully completing the assigned tasks.
- cooperative social skills by using these skills while engaged in group activities.
- positive interdependence by sharing common goals, rewards, and tasks with the group.
- group processing by reflecting on the group's progress, achievement, and success.

As Bellanca and Fogarty (2003) maintain, "If all five (of the above) are not present, students are not engaged in true cooperative learning. The characteristics operate as mental hooks to provide a framework for designing strong and effective cooperative learning tasks" (p. 7).

While cooperative learning is an instructional tool that can be used in a traditional learning format, Williams and Dunn (2008) point out that it is crucial for teaching in an extended time format because it provides for

- variety in the intensity of the instruction provided.
- student interaction.
- higher-order thinking.
- coverage of more material as students work in groups.

EFFECTIVE STRATEGIES FOR COOPERATIVE LEARNING

Jigsaw Groups

Jigsaw Groups (Aronson, Stephan, Sikes, Blaney, & Snapp, 1978; Slavin, 1994) enable students to learn new material using a cooperative team learning approach. In effect, the jigsaw process requires that each student on the team becomes an expert on a portion of a topic or reading the class is learning about. Each team member is then responsible for teaching the other team members about his or her section as well as learning the information other group members have to share. In order to accomplish this, students meet in "expert" groups to study their share of the topic or reading and, when finished, return to their home teams to teach and share their newly found knowledge.

Steps for Jigsaw Group Strategy

1. Select a unit of study that can be divided into the number of sections equal to the number of students in the home group. Sections should be chosen that students can complete in no more than 30 minutes.

2. Develop an "expert sheet" that establishes the parameters of the assignment, such as page numbers, purpose-setting questions, teacher expectations, et cetera.

3. Assign students to each section of the Jigsaw Group.

4. Allow students time to complete the reading for their assigned sections.

5. After completing the reading, have students with the same assigned segment meet together for approximately 20 minutes as an "expert group" to share the information and prepare a presentation for their group members.

6. Then have students meet with their home groups to listen and learn about the material from the "experts."

7. Finally, have students exhibit their newly found knowledge in discussion, by taking a quiz or test, or by completing a written response or project.

Figure 2.1 presents a graphic representation of the jigsaw method.

There is a variation on the jigsaw method presented above that works well for students who can comprehend assigned readings with ease. In this variation, students do not meet as an expert group, but, instead, each reads his or her assigned segment individually and then presents the information to the whole group. See Figure 2.2 for a graphic example of this variation.

Jigsaw Groups

Step One: Home Group reading segments assigned

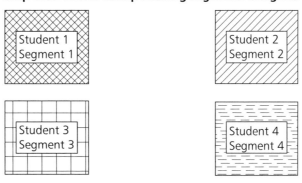

Step Two: Expert Group meets and discusses reading

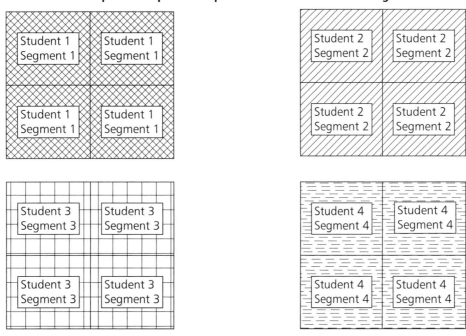

Step Three: Experts return to Home Group to share information

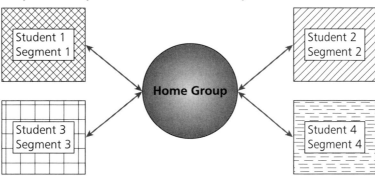

Figure 2.1

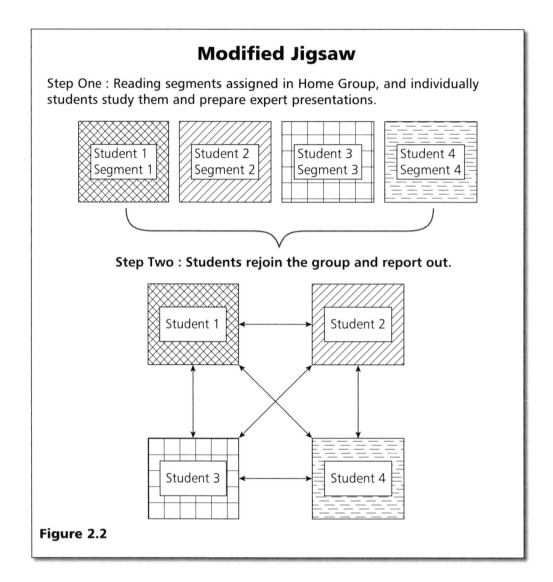

Modified Jigsaw

Step One : Reading segments assigned in Home Group, and individually students study them and prepare expert presentations.

Student 1
Segment 1

Student 2
Segment 2

Student 3
Segment 3

Student 4
Segment 4

Step Two : Students rejoin the group and report out.

Student 1

Student 2

Student 3

Student 4

Figure 2.2

Reciprocal Teaching

The Reciprocal Teaching strategy (Palincsar & Brown, 1986) fosters student instruction in four strategies that are critical to good comprehension: summarizing, asking questions, making predictions, and noting any difficulties in the materials. During Reciprocal Teaching, the teacher segments the text into small chunks, and, through a structured discussion format, students process the reading, periodically checking for understanding. At the conclusion of each segment of text, the students utilize the four comprehension strategies—summarizing, questioning, clarifying, and predicting—to facilitate their understanding. The strategy has been found to be most effective for motivating students to read (Carter, 1997; Palincsar & Herrenkohl, 2002) as well as for improving reading comprehension on standardized tests (Alfassi, 1998). However, it is important to note that for the strategy to be completely successful, teachers must model it and allow students to practice before they use the strategy in their cooperative groups.

Steps for Reciprocal Teaching Strategy

The steps for carrying out the Reciprocal Teaching strategy are as follows:

1. Begin with a section of content text that contains a series of well-written paragraphs.

2. Tell students that you are going to demonstrate four different strategies: summarizing, questioning, clarifying, and predicting.

3. Next, have the students silently read through the first paragraph of the reading. After the silent reading is completed, model the procedure according to the following format:

   a. **Summarize:** In a few sentences, summarize the gist of the selection, and explain how you developed your summary.

   b. **Question:** Ask the students an open-ended question about the paragraph's content. Avoid literal-level questions. Instead, strive to pose inferential or application questions.

   c. **Clarify:** Next, note any unfamiliar words or unclear statements in the paragraph, and comment about what you think they mean. Support your clarification by explaining, giving examples, or drawing analogies.

   d. **Predict:** Finally, make a prediction as to what you think will be learned in the next several paragraphs of the text.

4. Once students clearly understand the process, ask a student to be the teacher, and do the four-strategy sequence with the next paragraph or section of text. As the student plays "teacher," provide feedback, and encourage students to provide feedback about the questions, summaries, and predictions as well.

5. Continue the process by allowing students to take turns being the teacher until the reading assignment is complete.

6. Reinforce the strategy over a period of several days until students are comfortable with the process. When students are clearly comfortable with the process, they may work in small groups, thus fostering their reading independence.

See the blackline master, Figure 2.18 at the end of this chapter, for a role sheet that students may use to guide their discussion of each section of the strategy.

Student Teams Achievement Divisions (STAD)

Student Teams Achievement Divisions (STAD), developed by Robert Slavin (1994), is similar to the Jigsaw Group technique, since students engage in a cooperative team to learn material. In this strategy, however, students are first involved in a whole group presentation of the material to be taught, and then they process that information in a small group learning team activity.

Steps for Student Teams Achievement Divisions (STAD) Strategy

1. Develop worksheets that present questions, with answers, about the topic.
2. Next, introduce the topic to be studied to the entire class.
3. In their group, members then process the material together by
   a. discussing the material.
   b. comparing their answers to teacher-generated study materials.
   c. quizzing each other.
4. As a final step, students exhibit their newly found knowledge by taking a quiz or test or by completing a written response or project.

If a grade is desired for this activity, the teacher can issue both a team score, which is based on the team's improvement over past achievement, and an individual score, which is based on each student's performance.

Group Investigation Strategy

The Group Investigation strategy, developed by Sharan and Sharan (1992), engages students in working together to investigate key questions about a topic of mutual interest or a problem they need to solve. During the process, students (1) identify and define a topic or problem; (2) choose an aspect of the topic or problem to investigate; (3) gather, analyze, and synthesize information that relates to the topic or problem; (4) collect appropriate resources; (5) determine time to work together to investigate the topic or problem; and finally, (6) evaluate the success of their chosen investigation or solution.

Steps for Group Investigation Strategy

1. Introduce a broad topic or problem to be investigated.
2. Next, students brainstorm subtopics of the topic or problem.
3. Students choose the subtopic of interest to them and form their investigation groups accordingly.

4. In investigation groups, students determine
   a. how they will investigate their topic or problem.
   b. how they will divide the work.
   c. what outcomes they intend to achieve.
   d. what product(s) they will produce to show their results.

5. Next, each member of the investigation group gathers information, analyzes data, organizes information, suggests solutions, and reaches a conclusion.

6. When the research has been completed, individual members share their findings and collaborate on what findings they will present and what format they will utilize to present them.

7. Investigation groups then present their findings to the class.

8. The process concludes with self, peer, and teacher evaluations.

An adaptation: In some instances, students may decide to subdivide the original topic or problem. In that case, each group member investigates his or her aspect of the topic or problem, summarizes the findings, and makes a mini presentation of the findings to the class as part of the whole Group Investigation presentation.

MULTIPLE INTELLIGENCE THEORY

In 1983 Harvard psychologist Howard Gardner published the book *Frames of Mind*, which identified his theory of multiple intelligences and described seven intelligences, and in 1995 he identified an eighth intelligence. According to Gardner, every person possesses all eight of these intelligences at some level, and most people can develop each intelligence to an acceptable level of competency if that intelligence is awakened, amplified, and taught. As noted earlier, all children can learn; they just learn in different ways and according to different time frames.

As a result, and congruent with Williams and Dunn's (2008) eighth facet that learning occurs for the greatest number in an environment that fosters and accommodates various ways of being smart, teachers must provide multiple modalities for students, so they can engage in their learning in the most effective and productive ways. The use of activities based on the multiple intelligences helps to accomplish this by allowing students not only to learn in a variety of ways but also to show what they have learned in a variety of ways. Furthermore, as Csikszentmihalyi (1990) noted, when students are encouraged to develop new strengths, as they are when utilizing their multiple intelligences, they become more motivated, enjoy their work more, and seek a greater level of competence in that work. In effect, utilizing

Howard Gardner's multiple intelligence theory helps us remember that it is not "how smart we are, but how we are smart!" (ABC News, 1993).

What Are the Eight Intelligences?

According to Howard Gardner (1983), in order to be identified as an intelligence

> a human intellectual competence must entail a set of skills for problem solving—enabling the individual to resolve genuine problems or difficulties that he or she encounters and, when appropriate, to create an effective product—and must also entail the potential for finding or creating problems—thereby laying the groundwork for the acquisition of new knowledge. (pp. 60–61)

As noted earlier, Gardner has identified eight intelligences that all people possess.

1. Students who possess the **verbal/linguistic intelligence** are able to use all aspects of language easily and effectively. They enjoy reading, writing, listening, and speaking; they are skillful at completing word games, using and creating puns and jokes, and writing reports, essays, poems, and stories and communicating effectively through speeches and debates.

2. Students who possess the **logical/mathematical intelligence** are able to effectively manipulate numbers and use logic and reasoning skills. In addition, they utilize inductive and deductive thinking, enjoy mathematical and scientific reasoning, and deal with problem solving in a precise and methodical way.

3. Students who possess the **visual/spatial intelligence** see and accurately interpret what they see through the use of color, line, shape, form, and space. They like to draw, design, and build things and enjoy creating diagrams, maps, paintings, and three dimensional models.

4. Students who possess the **bodily/kinesthetic intelligence** use their entire bodies to express ideas and feelings and to produce products. They are extremely tactile, usually possess good eye-hand coordination, enjoy hands-on learning, and do well when asked to participate in performances, dramatization, and athletics.

5. Students who possess the **musical/rhythmic intelligence** are able to perceive, discriminate, and express a variety of musical forms. They respond enthusiastically to the sounds and rhythms they hear in the world, so they appreciate music and poetry and are skilled at composing songs and playing musical instruments.

6. Students who possess the **naturalist intelligence** focus on the world of nature and the diversity of its people. They seem to understand how the universe works and appreciate the intricacies it provides, such as the veins on leaves, the beauty of a carpet of grass, or how the tops of trees make a roof for a forest. Naturalists celebrate the notions of conservation and environmentalism.

7. Students who possess the **interpersonal intelligence** understand people and their moods, feelings, and motivations. Interpersonal students have exceptional social skills, and their charismatic nature allows them to work well with groups, while their enthusiasm for discussing ideas and building consensus often places them in leadership roles.

8. Students who possess the **intrapersonal intelligence** know themselves well and utilize that knowledge to grow both mentally and emotionally. They pay attention to their inner feelings, which in turn lead them to be introspective and reflective, so they are able to recognize their own specific strengths and weaknesses. As a result, they often prefer a solitary environment and reject offers to participate in group activities.

Like cooperative learning, multiple intelligences can be used as an instructional tool in a traditional learning format, but it, too, is crucial for teaching in an extended time format, because it incorporates so many of the facets identified by Williams and Dunn (2008) as brain-compatible because it

- makes learning personal (Facet 1).
- motivates the learner (Facet 2).
- provides for hands-on learning (Facet 3).
- encourages reflection (Facet 6).
- incorporates the students' senses and emotions (Facet 7).
- celebrates students' multiple intelligences (Facet 8).
- allows learning to be a high-energy activity (Facet 9).

The use of activities that utilize the multiple intelligences assures that all students will have the opportunity to learn in a manner that best suits them. Figure 2.3 provides a list of various multiple intelligence tasks. The blackline master, Figure 2.17 at the end of this chapter, depicts a method of planning for the use of the multiple intelligences in every unit taught, while Figure 2.4 provides an illustration of a multiple intelligences unit.

Tasks and Assessments for the Multiple Intelligences

Verbal/Linguistic	Logical/Mathematical	Visual/Spatial	Bodily/Kinesthetic

alphabetizing activities
choral speaking
class discussions
creative writing
debating
dramatic readings
essays
interviews
journals/logs/diaries
listening activities
literature circles
panel discussions
poetry
process writing
Readers' Theater
reading aloud
researching
retelling
speeches
story or report writing
storytelling
word games
Writers' Workshop
	cartoons
	collages
	designing posters
	drawing or making models
	filmmaking
	graphs, flow charts, and
	  other graphic images
	guided imagery
	making 3D projects
	making visual analogies
	making visual metaphors
	mind mapping
	murals
	painting
	photographing
	preparing visual stories
	sculpting
	sketching
	video tape or computer
	  presentations
	visual puzzles
		acting
		centers
		cooperative learning
		crafts
		creative movement
		dancing
		drama, charades
		dramatizing
		exploration/field trips
		hands-on experiments
		interviews
		investigations
		labs
		manipulatives
		miming
		physical education
		physical exercise
		scavenger hunts
		science experiments
		simulations
		sports/games
			analogies
			brain teasers, logic games
			calculating or computing
			categorizing facts
			classifying
			collecting data
			critical thinking activities
			experiments and labs
			following recipes
			graphic organizers
			interpreting patterns
			lateral thinking
			outlining
			problem solving
			puzzles
			research projects
			scientific experiments
			sequencing
			solving puzzles
			story problems
			surveys
			time lines
			using geometry

Musical/Rhythmic	Interpersonal	Intrapersonal	Naturalist

background music
choral readings
cinquains, haiku, cheers,
  jingles, raps, poems
compose songs
create raps
drawing/writing
  to music
keeping time to a beat
making instruments
mnemonics
music in nature
musical games
playing an instrument
rhyming
singing songs
studying musicians
tapping out poetic
  rhythms
writing lyrics
	brainstorming
	choral readings
	class discussions
	character webs
	cooperative activities
	cooperative learning
	debating
	group work
	interviewing
	sharing
	jigsawing information
	peer editing
	peer teaching
	problem solving
	role-playing
	Socratic dialogue
	speeches
	teaching or helping others
	working in teams
		autobiographies
		reflective journals,
		  diaries, logs
		editorials
		family tree
		independent projects
		independent reading
		individual study
		personal choice in
		  projects
		personal goal setting
		personal response
		personal timelines
		personalized contracts
		poetry
		self-reflection
			animal watching
			bird watching
			build a garden
			classifying or identifying
			collecting rocks
			creating a habitat
			dissecting
			experimenting
			going to the zoo
			graphic organizers
			identifying plants
			nature walk
			photo layout
			picture poster
			read, study outdoors
			record data
			study clouds
			study stars
			use a microscope
			weather forecasting

Figure 2.3

Multiple Intelligence Planning Sheet

Goals for Lesson:

1.

2.

3.

4.

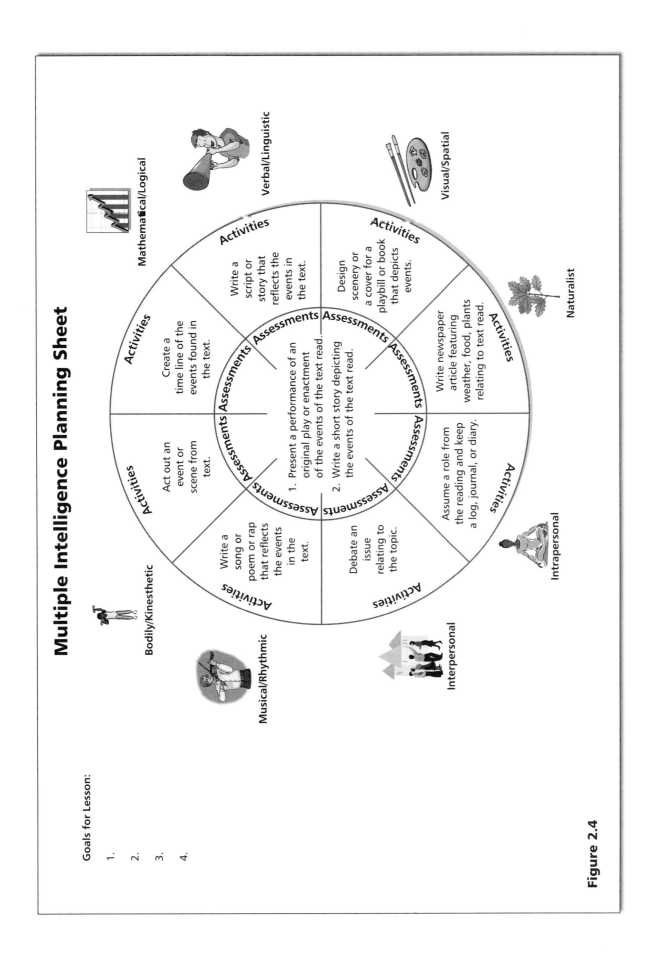

Mathematical/Logical

Verbal/Linguistic

Visual/Spatial

Naturalist

Bodily/Kinesthetic

Musical/Rhythmic

Interpersonal

Intrapersonal

Activities

Create a time line of the events found in the text.

Write a script or story that reflects the events in the text.

Design scenery or a cover for a playbill or book that depicts events.

Write newspaper article featuring weather, food, plants relating to text read.

Act out an event or scene from text.

Write a song or poem or rap that reflects the events in the text.

Debate an issue relating to the topic.

Assume a role from the reading and keep a log, journal, or diary.

Assessments

1. Present a performance of an original play or enactment of the events of the text read.

2. Write a short story depicting the events of the text read.

Figure 2.4

EFFECTIVE QUESTIONING TECHNIQUES

As far back as 1979, Delores Durkin determined that, as teachers, we use questioning more than any other method to ascertain whether our students understand what they read. Unfortunately, according to Busching and Slesinger (1995) and Armbruster et al. (1991), we, as teachers, also dominate the questioning process, generating all the questions and requiring students to generate few. In addition, we fall into what Richardson and Morgan (2003) refer to as traps when we develop the questions we ask our students. One trap they describe is that we often ask students questions before they have had an opportunity to process what they have read. Fisher and Frey (2008) note, "Questioning loses its effectiveness when teachers require students to swallow and regurgitate facts before they have had an opportunity to chew and digest the information" (p. 102). Another trap Richardson and Morgan (2003) present is that the questions teachers ask most often are literal in type and require no critical thinking, and this concern is echoed by several others (Durkin, 1979; Sturtevant, 1992; Wimer, Ridenour, & Thomas, 2001; Young & Daines, 1992). In fact, Guszak (1967) found that 78% of questions asked of second graders, 65% of questions asked of fourth graders, and 58% of questions asked of sixth graders were at the literal level. Gall (1984) reported that only 20% of the questions asked in classrooms are at a level higher than the literal level, while Knight (2005), after observing over 1,000 classrooms, discovered that more than 75% of the questions asked were at the knowledge level, the lowest level on Bloom's taxonomy. As a result, one can easily conclude that if students are consistently asked questions at the literal level and provided little opportunity to answer questions at the inferential and application levels, their ability to respond effectively to higher-level questions is diminished. This is, perhaps, the reason why so often students will complain that the answer to a question in their study guide or chapter review is just not to be found in the book. As a result, having passed through an elementary school experience drenched in literal-level questions, students come to expect them as they journey through middle and high school. In effect, they expect to be served up only literal-level questions, because that is all they have ever experienced.

Yet another trap that teachers fall into when questioning comes from the work of Cazden (2001), Dillon (2004), and Mehan (1979), who determined that most questioning that occurs in classrooms follows the IRE cycle: **I**nitiate, **R**espond, **E**valuate. In this pattern of questions, the teacher initiates the question, students respond to the question, and the teacher evaluates whether the question has been answered correctly. This format of inquiry, however, leads to a passive learning environment where, as Mehan tells us, the teacher decides who, besides herself or himself, will speak. Instead of such a passive environment, students need an active environment where they are plied with inferential and application questions and allowed to generate their own questions, especially divergent ones (Crapse, 1995). In fact, both Ciardello (1998) and Oakes and Lipton (1999) stress that when students are allowed to develop their own questions, they will develop a higher level of understanding of what they are studying.

Thus, it is crucial that, as students enter middle and high school, they receive practice in answering higher-level questions. However, it must be noted that since a majority of students in middle school and high school have had little practice in higher-level questioning, teachers must not only employ effective questioning strategies, but they must model the inquiry process as well. Information on what constitutes effective questions, how to construct effective questions, and strategies to help students employ higher-level questioning strategies is provided in the sections below.

CONSTRUCTING GOOD QUESTIONS

Good questions are essential to effective learning. They help arouse student curiosity and interest in the topic they will study, set forth and clarify the key concepts to be learned, and, if constructed well, will help students think more critically and problem solve more effectively. A first step in developing good questions to ask is to be sure that the questions will require students to use the thinking skills they are trying to develop, and this can be accomplished if the teacher is acquainted with a system for organizing those thinking skills such as Bloom's Taxonomy, a classification system that describes six levels of competence and that was revised in 2001 by Anderson and Krathwohl. While the revised taxonomy is similar to the original, there are three major changes. First, while the elements of the original taxonomy were written as nouns, the elements of the revised taxonomy are written as verbs. Second, within each cognitive dimension, specific cognitive processes are listed. Finally, the order of the last two levels of Bloom's original taxonomy has been reversed in the revised edition. See Figure 2.5.

Bloom's Taxonomy as Revised by Anderson and Krathwohl

Questioning Category	Bloom's Category	Student Activity	Typical Stem Words	Example
Lower level	Remember	State facts, terms definitions, concepts, etc., and repeat them.	List Name Define Describe Find	What are the major causes of global warming?
Lower level	Understand	Understand material by explaining its meaning and intent.	Explain Interpret Summarize Paraphrase Predict Translate Classify	Explain the process of photosynthesis.
Lower level	Apply	Apply previously learned knowledge and skills to new situations.	Implement Solve Apply Modify Construct Execute	Based on your knowledge of osmosis and diffusion, explain how mummification was carried out.
Higher level	Analyze	Break material down into component parts, and infer causes or motives.	Compare ____ to ____. How does ____ apply? Why does ____ work?	What global factors are affecting the current price of gasoline?
Higher level	Evaluate	Use specific criteria to make judgments and defend opinions.	What criteria would you use to ____? What judgments can you make? What hypothesis can you make? Critique the ____.	How effective is the symbolism in *The Red Badge of Courage?*
Higher level	Create	Hypothesize, predict, generalize, put parts together to create, or develop something original.	Can you design a ____? How would you create a ____? What plan can you develop for solving ____?	What steps would you need to follow to design a successful campaign for student council president?

Figure 2.5

Source: Adapted from Anderson and Krathwohl (2001).

Bloom's revised six-level taxonomy is often divided into low- and high-level questions with the knowledge, comprehension, and application levels of the taxonomy denoted as low level, and analysis, synthesis, and evaluation denoted as high level. Basically, we use lower-level questions to (1) evaluate students' preparation and comprehension, (2) diagnose students' strengths and weaknesses, and (3) review or summarize content; and we use higher-level questions to encourage students to (1) think deeply and critically, (2) problem solve, (3) engage in discussions, and (4) seek information on their own (Center for Teaching Excellence, 2007a).

In addition to being classified as low or high, questions may also be classified as *closed* or *open* (Center for Teaching Excellence, 2007a). Closed and open questions may exist at any level of the taxonomy. A closed question is a question that has a limited number of possible answers, and, in most cases, the teacher is cognizant of all the possible answers the student might give. An example of a lower-level closed question is, "Where did the first battle of the Civil War occur?" while a higher-level closed question is, "What are the artistic elements of a landscape painting?" An open question is a question that has many possible acceptable answers, and teachers may not be cognizant of all the possible answers the student will provide. An example of a lower-level open question is, "What are some ways we might combat global warming?" while an example of a higher-level open question is, "Design a plan to eliminate the effects of global warming in the next five years."

To be effective questioners, teachers need to carefully prepare their questions before asking them of their students. The Center for Teaching Excellence (2007b), on its Web page, Planning Questions, provides some clear suggestions for planning questions.

- Write all main questions in advance.
- Select the content for questioning. Choose material you consider important and have emphasized during class rather than trivial material.
- Identify the goal or purpose for asking the question. In other words do you want to measure the students' knowledge of facts? Application? Comprehension? Ability to evaluate?
- Your goal or purpose should help you determine what levels of questions you will ask. Do you want recall? Analysis? Generation of a new idea? Be sure to use an appropriate variety and mix of questions utilizing all levels of Bloom's taxonomy.
- Phrase questions carefully and concisely. Avoid questions that can be answered "yes" or "no," and, instead, ask questions that require an extended response.
- Phrase questions clearly so students understand the task. Avoid "guess what I am thinking" questions like, "Name the greatest artist of the Renaissance era." This question has several possible correct

answers, and the teacher must probe to get the one he or she considers the correct one.

- Avoid posing a question that contains the answer, such as, "Don't you agree that *Othello* was the worst of Shakespeare's tragedies?"
- When planning your questions, try to anticipate possible student responses. Doing this will help you determine if the questions are phrased accurately and focused on the identified goal or purpose.
- Arrange the list of questions in a logical sequence, such as from specific to general or lower level to higher level, or a sequence related to the content you are inquiring about.
- Ask questions of the entire group rather than focusing on individual students. This will keep all students attentive and engaged.
- Provide sufficient wait time. Giving students time to think enhances their analytic and problem solving skills. Ideally, teachers should wait three to five seconds before calling for an answer.
- Listen carefully to what students say in their responses. Acknowledge correct answers with positive reinforcement and incorrect responses with probing questions to gently guide the student to an appropriate or correct response.

As with cooperative learning and the use of multiple intelligences, the use of higher order questioning is an instructional tool that can be used in a traditional learning format, but it, too, is crucial for teaching in an extended time format. This is due primarily to the fact that an extended time period allows for students to truly discuss rather than merely recite. And, as Walsh and Sattes (2005) clarify, discussion, as opposed to mere recitation, provides students an opportunity to think out loud and express their thoughts and beliefs, respond to diverse points of view, formulate hypotheses, present supporting evidence, and, finally, make connections and transfer what they have learned to new applications.

QUESTIONING STRATEGIES

Once teachers have successfully developed their questioning skills, they must hone their students' inquiry skills as well. The following strategies will accomplish this.

Question-Answer Relationship (QAR) Strategy

How many times have you heard your students complain that they have been given questions on a study guide or at the end of a chapter for which they cannot locate the answers? Raphael, Au, and Highfield (2006) suggest that this situation occurs because students have not been given guidance in knowing how to answer questions. In order to combat this problem, Raphael developed the Question-Answer Relationship (QAR) strategy, which enables students to recognize three types of questions: the "right there," or textually explicit question, that is found easily in one place in the text; the "think and search," or textually implicit question, which students must think about and peruse several sections of the text to answer; and, finally, the "author and you" and "on your own" questions, which students must answer by processing and applying what they know and have learned and by transferring their knowledge to real-life applications. See Figure 2.6 for an example of the characteristics of the four types of QAR questions.

Steps for QAR Strategy

1. Introduce the concept of QAR by explaining each type of question, providing a clear example of each, and discussing the difference in each.

2. Next, assign a short piece of text for students to read.

3. Upon completion of the reading, lead the students through the process of answering each type of question, making sure they go back into the text to verify their answers. Ascertain that they clearly understand the differences among each type.

Characteristics of the Four Types of QAR Questions

Kind of Question	Textually Explicit or Implicit	Characteristics
Right there	Explicit	Answer stated directly in the text.
Think and search	Implicit	Answer requires students to put together several sections of the text.
Author and you	Explicit and implicit	Answer requires that students mesh their thoughts about a topic with information the author presents.
On your own	Implicit	Answer comes from application of the information from the text.

Figure 2.6

4. Continue this practice, increasing the number of questions of each type, until students are clearly able to understand the differences among the types and can identify them with ease.

5. Finally, ask students to read a longer passage and develop a set of questions for their classmates to identify and answer.

When students have become accustomed to the QAR format, they can easily apply the strategy to content area assignments and discussion sessions. Once my students became familiar with QAR, I was able to aid students having difficulty locating an answer to a question with a simple reminder like, "It is a think and search question," or "It is an on your own question." Often the student would respond immediately with, "Oh! Now I get it!" See Figure 2.7 for an example of QAR strategy in the social studies classroom and Figure 2.8 for an example of QAR strategy in a science classroom.

Example of QAR Strategy for Social Studies

The American Revolution

Right There Questions

1. How did the colonists react to the Stamp Act?
2. Who were the Sons of Liberty?

Think and Search Questions

1. Who attended the Boston Tea Party?
2. What were some famous firsts that were initiated during the revolutionary period in America?

Author and You Questions

1. Why did the new American nation prefer a weak rather than a strong central government?
2. Why was it so difficult for John Adams to negotiate a trade treaty with Britain?

On Your Own Questions

1. During the Revolutionary War period, the Patriots were a minority. Did they have the right to act for the larger majority that preferred to remain loyal to Britain? Explain your answer.
2. During the Revolution, the British won cities but lost the war. Why was that possible? Could that happen today?

Figure 2.7

Example of QAR Strategy for Science

Planet Mars

Right There Questions

    1. How long is a year on Mars?

    2. What is the temperature on Mars?

Think and Search Questions

    1. How is Mars different from Earth?

    2. What makes Mars a terrestrial planet?

Author and You Questions

    1. How were scientists able to learn new information about Mars?

    2. Why do you think Mars was named as it was?

On Your Own Questions

    1. Do you think there is life on Mars? Explain your answer.

    2. Describe what you think life on Mars would be like.

Figure 2.8

Questioning the Author

An especially effective strategy for helping students interact with their content area reading texts and create meaning by analyzing the author's purpose rather than merely attending to what the texts say is Questioning the Author (Beck, McKeown, Hamilton, & Kucan, 1997). This strategy addresses the problem that results because the textbooks our students read are not always user friendly. In effect, they do not always take into consideration the fact that not all students possess the appropriate level of prior knowledge needed to comprehend the concepts presented, and thus the information these texts provide may not be explained as fully as students need. As a result, the information these texts present may be confusing to the student.

In order to combat this problem, Beck, McKeown, Hamilton, and Kucan (1997) suggest that teachers pose questions or queries to serve as discussion prompts to enable students to become responsible for their thinking and thus construct meaning for themselves. During this process, the teacher participates by acting not only as a facilitator and guide but also as one who initiates questions and sometimes responds to them, all the while making certain to uphold the goals of Questioning the Author, which are to help students (1) construct meaning from the text's content, (2) transcend the words on the page, and (3) make connections to real-life experiences.

Steps for Questioning the Author

1. First the teacher must read the text to be studied closely and determine the major concepts students should learn as well as any problems they might encounter in understanding these concepts due to text complexity or difficulty.

2. Next teachers must determine how the text will be segmented for student reading. In other words, at what points in the text will the students stop reading and begin discussion to question the author. A way to effectively segment text is to pay attention to where major concepts occur or where difficult or confusing text emerges and to segment the text at those points.

3. Once the text is segmented, the queries to be asked of the author must be developed. These queries are designed to be used during reading to help students focus on the quality and depth of their understanding of the text as well as facilitate discussion and interaction between students. Beck, McKeown, Hamilton, and Kucan (1997) describe three levels of queries: (1) initiating queries and (2) follow-up queries, which are designed to be used with expository text, and (3) narrative queries, which are designed to be used with narrative text. Examples and a fuller explanation of these queries are found in Figure 2.9.

4. To effectively implement this strategy, teachers need to prepare students to question the author by helping them establish and understand who the author is. To accomplish this, students must think of the author as a participant in their discussion, so effective questions to pose to students might be the following: Who is talking to you in this book? What expertise does the author have? Why do you think this author wanted to write this text?

5. Once students understand who the author is, they need to learn how to effectively question that author by utilizing the self-questioning process. This process is best modeled by the teacher, who chooses a passage from the text and proceeds to think the reading through

aloud by noting what made the reading easy, difficult, or confusing and by identifying what concepts the author expects the reader to know and understand.

6. Once the implementation of the strategy begins, the teacher plays an active role by asking open-ended questions, affirming key points, paraphrasing or summarizing student commentaries, and even providing supplementary information for clarification of unclear material, if necessary.

7. As students become facile with this strategy, they can be encouraged to generate their own queries. Working alone or in a small group, students can segment their text and generate appropriate queries.

Question the Author Queries

Expository Queries

Goal of Query	Possible Queries
Initiate a discussion.	1. What do you think the author is trying to say in this reading? 2. What do you think is the message the author is giving you? 3. What do you think the author is really talking about?
Follow up to focus on 1. what the author meant. 2. making connections. 3. why the author presents certain information and ideas.	1. What do you think the author means in his text? 2. Do you think the author explains his ideas clearly in his writing? 3. Does what the author says in this passage make sense with what she has said before? 4. How does what the author says here help you connect to what you have learned before? 5. Why do you think the author includes the information he does?

Narrative Queries

Goal of Query	Possible Queries
Examine characters and their motivations.	1. Based on what you have read, what is the author telling you about the character and his or her situation? 2. What hints can you get from what the author has told you to help you predict what the character will do next?
Examine how the plot is crafted.	1. What information does the author present that helps you figure out that things have changed for the character? 2. How does the author bring the events in the plot to a close?

Figure 2.9

Source: Based on suggestions for questions provided by Beck, McKeown, Hamilton, and Kucan (1997, pp. 37–42).

ReQuest

The ReQuest procedure (Manzo, 1969) is designed to improve students' reading comprehension by developing their questioning behaviors. During the process, students are encouraged to ask questions about text material and to set their own purposes for reading. This procedure is indirectly diagnostic, since by noting the kinds of questions the students ask, the teacher can determine whether students are comprehending. In addition, through teacher modeling of good questioning behaviors, students gain insight into how good readers question themselves as they read.

Steps for the ReQuest Procedure

1. Both the students and the teacher silently read a common selection from the text. The selection can be read one sentence at a time or a paragraph at a time.
2. After they have all read the passage, the students ask the teacher as many questions as they can. The teacher answers the questions clearly and completely, thus modeling appropriate, complete answers.
3. Next, the teacher asks the students questions about the same sentence or paragraph, and the students answer as fully as possible. In this way, the teacher can model good questioning strategies.
4. When the students have finished answering, the teacher and students read the next sentence or paragraph and proceed as before.
5. When the students have processed enough information to make predictions about the rest of the selection, the exchange of questions stops.
6. As students become comfortable with the process, they may gradually increase the amount of text read and may work in pairs or in small groups, thus fostering their reading independence.

Socratic Questioning

Another effective strategy for engaging students in good questioning techniques is Socratic Questioning. For most students, classroom discussions are a time to answer the teacher's questions with a brief response, while such discussions should be, instead, an opportunity for students to delve into, reflect upon, and extend the concepts presented in the question in a lively, animated, high-level conversation. In effect, students need to learn to ask why, to explore their own personal beliefs about a concept, and to listen, analyze, and reflect upon what others say about that concept and respond accordingly. Furthermore, according to Ball (1996), students who utilize the Socratic Questioning technique actually participate 97% of the time in class discussions. The Socratic dialogue strategy, based on Socrates' belief that students must learn to think for themselves rather than just get the right answer, encourages critical thinking.

Steps for Socratic Questioning

1. Students read a text rich in ideas, issues, and values, which will stimulate thought and dialogue.

2. To get ready for the Socratic Questioning procedure, have a team of 10 to 12 students sit in a circle.

3. Next, establish the ground rules for the process, which should include the following:

    a. You may refer to the text when needed during the discussion.
    b. You may pass when asked to contribute.
    c. Do not participate if you are not prepared.
    d. If you are confused at any time, ask for clarification.
    e. Stick only to the idea currently under discussion; make notes about ideas you want to come back to.
    f. You do not need to raise your hand to contribute; instead, take turns speaking.
    g. Listen carefully.
    h. Speak loudly enough so that all can hear you.
    i. Talk to one another and not just to the leader or teacher.
    j. Discuss ideas rather than each other's opinions.
    k. Students can disagree with others in a respectful manner.

    Source: Adams (n.d.).

4. After reading, the dialogue is opened with a question, which may be posed by the leader or any of the participants. This question has no official correct answer, but, instead, leads the students into thoughtful reflection and new questions. As a result, students should ask each other follow-up or new questions as they arise in the discussion. The questions should require students to analyze, synthesize, or apply the information presented in the reading. Possible question types include the following:

    a. world connection question: a question connecting the text read to the real world

  b. close-ended question: a question regarding the text that will lead students to come to an agreement about the events or the characters in the text

  c. open-ended question: a question that requires students to logically think about the text in order to discover the answer

  d. universal theme or core question: a question that explores the universal truth presented in the text

  e. literary analysis question: a question that asks students to consider how an author composed a literary piece or how the author manipulated the point of view, the characters, the form, et cetera to create the work

Source: Adams (n.d.).

5. Students should provide evidence for each statement they make and identify its source.

6. Each student should participate. The discussion might begin with a round robin so that each student has an initial opportunity to participate.

7. The success of the discussion depends on the students' abilities to read analytically, listen carefully, reflect on the questions asked, and ask critical, thought-provoking questions in response.

Examples of Socratic Questions

Fogarty (2001) provides an extensive list of questions that are effective in Socratic Questioning:

What reasons do you have for saying that?

Why do you agree or disagree with that point?

How are you defining the term?

What do you mean by that expression?

Is what you're saying now consistent with what you said before?

Could you clarify that comment?

When you said that, what was implied by your remarks?

What follows from what you just said?

Is it possible that you are contradicting each other?

Could you clarify that remark?

Are you sure that you are not contradicting yourself?

What alternatives are there?

Could you give an example of that?

Are you familiar with incidents of this sort?

Why did you find that interesting?

Are you saying . . . ?

I wonder if what you're saying is . . . ?

So, you see it as . . . ?

Is that the point you're making?

Can I sum up what you've said by . . . ?

Are you suggesting . . . ?

If you're correct, would it follow . . . ?

The implications of what you've said seem far-reaching; if . . . then . . . ?

Aren't you assuming . . . ?

Is what you've just said based on . . . ?

What is your reason for saying that . . . ?

Why do you believe . . . ?

What can you say in defense of that view?

How do you know?

Couldn't it also be . . . ?

What if someone . . . ?

Source: From *Brain-Compatible Classrooms* (2nd ed., p. 103), by Robin Fogarty, 2002, Thousand Oaks, CA: Corwin. Copyright © 2002 by Corwin. Reprinted with permission.

GRAPHIC ORGANIZERS

Graphic organizers are powerful tools that facilitate comprehension and understanding. Marzano, Pickering, and Pollack (2001) remind us of the "dual-coding" theory of information storing that suggests that knowledge can be stored in two forms, a linguistic form and an imagery form. It is the imagery form, the form of storing knowledge in mental pictures or graphic organizers, that has been shown to stimulate and increase brain activity, and, in fact, using nonlinguistic representations such as graphic organizers actually motivates students to elaborate on the knowledge they possess, thereby understanding it in greater depth and recalling it with greater ease.

In addition, nonlinguistic representations, such as graphic organizers, help students visualize the structure of the text they are reading and enable them to organize their thinking while they are reading as well as record their knowledge when they have finished reading. Alvermann and Van Arnam (1984) as cited in Fisher and Frey (2008) discovered that, when utilizing graphic organizers, students reread text passages in order to clarify their understanding, and Alvermann and Boothby (1982) as cited in Fisher and Frey reported that the use of graphic organizers prompted students to practice active reading. In addition, Vacca (2002) reminds us that the use of graphic organizers helps students better comprehend expository texts because they allow the students to visually track organizational text patterns such as compare/contrast, problem/solution, and cause and effect. Furthermore, Vacca stresses that "graphic organizers enable students to identify what ideas in an expository text are important, how these ideas are related, and where to find specific information about these ideas in the text" (p. 10). Ellis (2004) agrees, noting that graphic organizers not only help students differentiate between essential and nonessential information but also, because they help students identify key information, reduce the processing demands made upon the students, thus facilitating learning of high-level content and use of high-level thinking.

Another valuable aspect of graphic organizers is that they can be used in any of the three stages of the learning process. Before learning begins, graphic organizers can be used to foster students' prior knowledge as well as to alert them as to what they will encounter in their reading, much like an advance organizer. As learning progresses, students can utilize graphic organizers as a note-taking tool by either completing a teacher-created organizer or by creating one of their own as they read the text material. Finally, students can complete a graphic organizer as an after-learning exercise by recording what has been learned.

As with cooperative learning, the use of multiple intelligences, and the use of higher-order questioning, the use of graphic organizers is an instructional tool that can be used in a traditional learning format, but it, too, is crucial for teaching in an extended time format. It addresses several of the facets identified by Williams and Dunn (2008) as brain-compatible, because it

- provides for hands-on learning (Facet 3).
- links new information to prior knowledge (Facet 4).

- incorporates chunked learning (Facet 5).
- encourages reflection (Facet 6).
- incorporates students' senses and emotions (Facet 7).
- celebrates students' multiple intelligences (Facet 8).

Willis (2007) further substantiates this connection to brain-based learning by noting that graphic organizers allow students to utilize the brain's innate search for patterns because they help students cluster or chunk materials. This, in turn, enables them to access prior knowledge, see relationships, relect upon the relationships they have made, make connections, determine patterns, and store new learning in long-term memory. In fact, Whiteley (2005) suggests that graphic organizers actually represent how students store knowledge in the brain. Finally, if graphic organizers are well designed, they engage students' positive emotions and creative abilities, so the students can begin to discover patterns for themselves.

Types of Graphic Organizers

Graphic organizers come in a variety of forms and are called by a myriad of names. Fisher and Frey (2008), however, have categorized all graphic organizers into four categories: (1) concept maps, (2) flow diagrams, (3) tree diagrams, and (4) matrices. Concept maps are basically lines and bubbles (or other shapes) that record the relationship between the main idea of a topic and its subtopics, or minor ideas, and are best used to explore shared attributes of a topic. Flow diagrams are ideal for recording a succession of information and allowing students to make sequential connections, as would be seen in flow charts, time lines, and storyboards. Tree diagrams are best used to categorize and classify material and usually radiate from general to specific, most important to least important, or something similar. This type of organizer illustrates how information is prioritized or ranked and often records processes, events, and time lines. Matrices, the final graphic organizer type, are used to classify, compare, and contrast and are useful in helping students analyze and classify data, draw conclusions, and make inferences. See Figure 2.10 for examples of the various graphic organizers.

Examples of Graphic Organizers

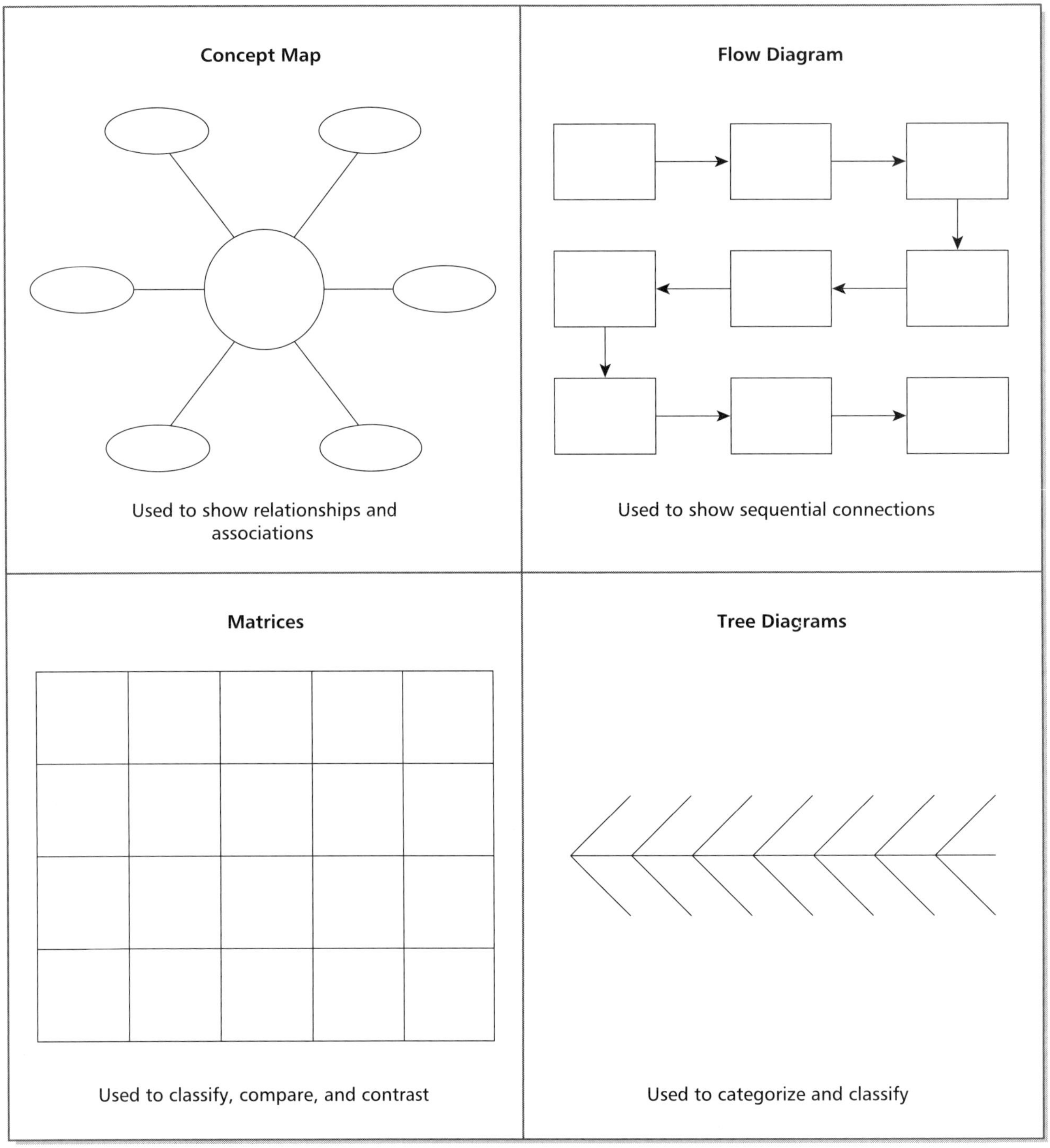

Concept Map

Used to show relationships and associations

Flow Diagram

Used to show sequential connections

Matrices

Used to classify, compare, and contrast

Tree Diagrams

Used to categorize and classify

Figure 2.10

Structured Note Taking

An especially valuable use of graphic organizers is to help students decipher the structure of the text they are reading. Richgels, McGee, Lomas, and Sheard (1987) and Taylor (1980) note that strategic readers regularly use text organization to give them a framework for finding, organizing, and interpreting important information. Structured Note Taking (Smith & Tompkins, 1988) is an effective strategy to help students learn organizational patterns, since the graphic organizer represents the reading selection's major text patterns.

Steps for Structured Note Taking

1. To better assist your students, preview the selection to be read to determine the organizational pattern used to convey the information.

2. Next, create a graphic organizer that follows this pattern, complete with focusing questions, and distribute it as a study guide.

3. Finally, instruct students to read the chapter and take notes by recording the appropriate information in the graphic organizer sections.

As time goes on, students will become adroit at spotting text organizational patterns and will be able to construct their own graphic organizers to record information. However, to facilitate this process, Buehl (2001) developed a set of focusing questions to guide students in determining the structure that texts utilize. Based on Buehl's questions, I have developed organizers for the five most common text structures used in expository writing, and figures 2.12 through 2.16 provide blackline masters for these organizers. Figure 2.11 shows how this strategy can be used for science class.

Problem/Solution Organizer

What is the problem?

Endangerment of Common Loon in
United States and Canada

Who has the problem?

Canadian provinces
U.S. states: Maine, Minnesota,
Wisconsin, Michigan's Upper
Peninsula

What causes the problem?

| Water sports on lakes and rivers | Lake pollution due to acid rain and waste dumping | Fishermen using lead sinkers (lead poisoning) |

What are effects?

| Decreased loon chick birth rate | Early death of loons |

What is result?

Diminished loon population

What is solution?

| Restrict water sports | Control industrial waste |

New Problem?

Decreased tourism

Figure 2.11

CHAPTER SUMMARY

Once the curriculum has been mapped and the lesson format finalized, teachers must search out those techniques that will most effectively and efficiently help them deliver the curriculum and lessons they will teach. Specifically, this chapter provides a discussion of (1) cooperative learning and strategies that utilize it, such as Jigsaw Groups, Reciprocal Teaching, and Student Teams Achievement Divisions (STAD); (2) brain-compatible strategies, with a specific focus on utilizing John Gardner's theory of multiple intelligences; (3) effective questioning techniques and strategies, such as question and answer relationship, Questioning the Author, ReQuest, and Socratic Questioning, and (4) graphic organizers and the Structured Note Taking strategy that utilizes them.

BLACKLINE MASTERS

Blackline masters for implementing the strategies in this chapter may be found on pages 60 through 66.

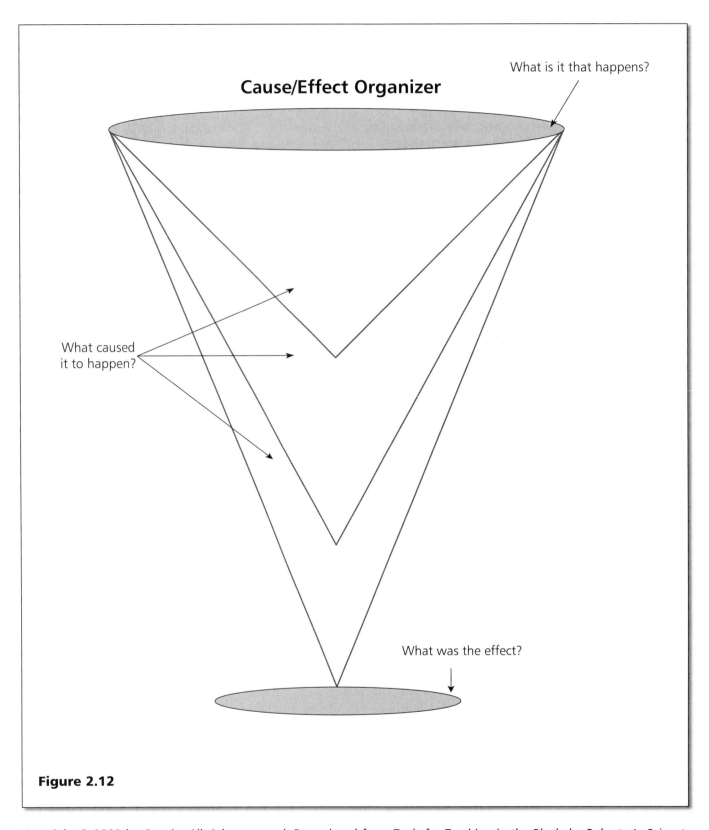

Figure 2.12

Comparison – Contrast Organizer

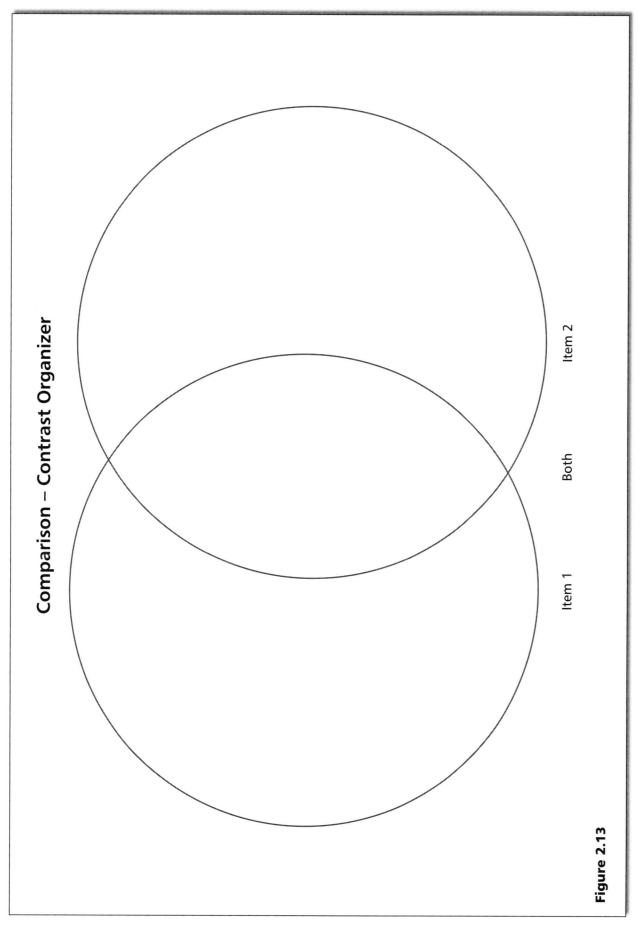

Item 1   Both   Item 2

Figure 2.13

Problem/Solution Organizer

What is the problem?

Who has the problem?

What causes the problem?

What are effects?   **What is solution?**   **What are the results?**

New problem?

Figure 2.14

Source: Based on questions developed by Buehl (2001).

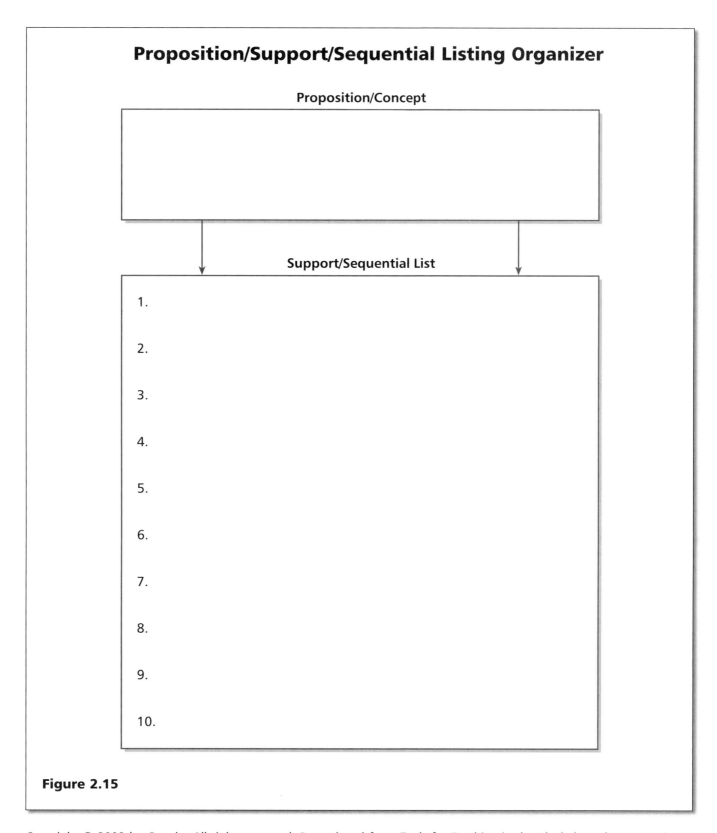

Proposition/Support/Sequential Listing Organizer

Proposition/Concept

Support/Sequential List

1.

2.

3.

4.

5.

6.

7.

8.

9.

10.

Figure 2.15

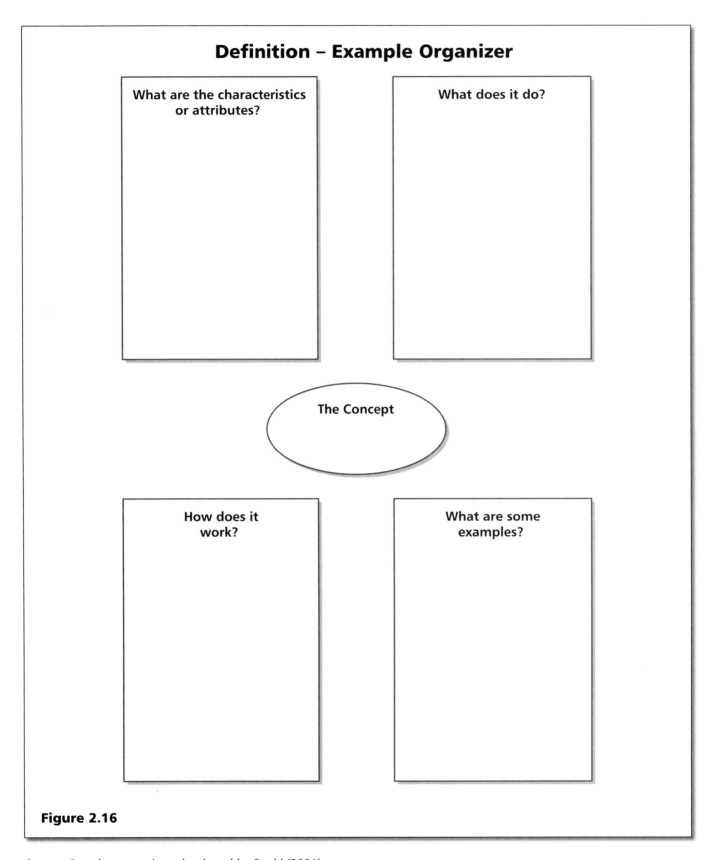

Figure 2.16

Source: Based on questions developed by Buehl (2001).

Multiple Intelligence Unit

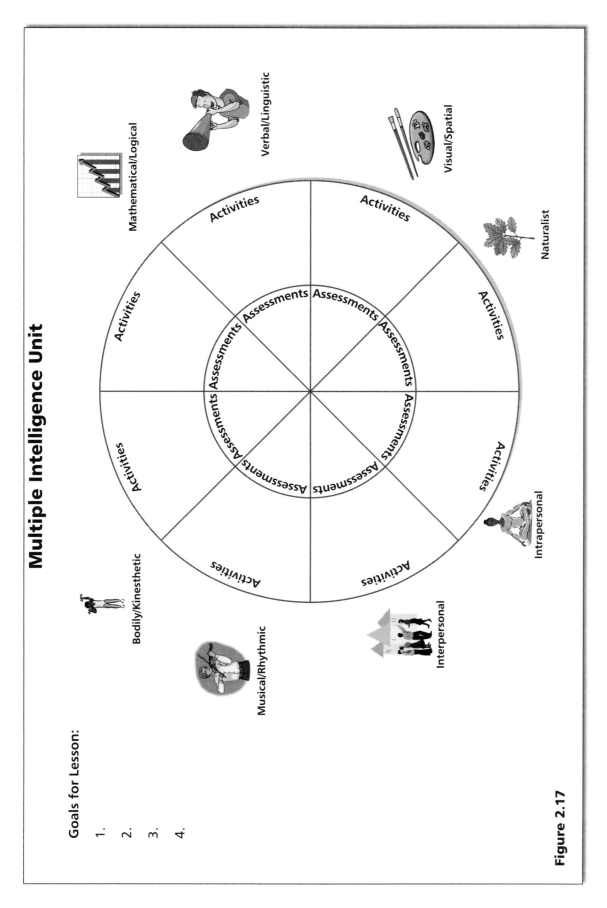

Goals for Lesson:

1.
2.
3.
4.

Figure 2.17

Reciprocal Teaching Role Sheet

Summarize

- What is the gist of what you read?
- What are the big ideas in your reading?
- What was the main or key idea of your reading?
- What details support that main idea?

Clarify

- What sections of the reading were confusing? Why?
- What words are hard for you to understand?
- What parts of the reading were hard for you to read? Why?
- Was there any idea or thought that was confusing to you? Tell about it.

Question

- How does what you read connect to you?
- How does it connect with your experience?
- How does it connect to something you have read or seen?
- Create a question using the following stem:

  I wonder . . . .
  I believe . . . .
  I think . . . .

Predict

- What do you think is going to happen in the next section of your reading?
- What do you think you will read about or learn in the next section of your reading?
- What are some of the clues that help you make this prediction?

Figure 2.18

CHAPTER 3

Entice the Learner

Only the curious will learn and only the resolute overcome the obstacles to learning.

—Eugene S. Wilson

THE FIRST PHASE: ENTICEMENT

An effective way to design a lesson plan for learning in the block is to follow a format that has four phases, each varying in time from 10 to 25 minutes. The first phase, Entice the Learner, lasts approximately 10 to 15 minutes and is grounded in the facets of a brain-compatible classroom as outlined by Williams and Dunn (2008) and discussed in Chapter 2, specifically facets 2, 4, 5, 7, and 9. The purpose of this phase is to make students aware of what they already know about a topic or subject and then help them foster adequate prior knowledge so they are mentally ready for instruction. In addition, it helps them identify a purpose for learning and clarifies, or even preteaches, the vocabulary and content demands that the text will make. Most important, however, it piques student interest in the learning and establishes questions that the lesson will cover, thus serving as a valuable motivational technique.

As discussed in Chapter 1, motivation to learn is certainly a challenge to today's students. In fact, researchers have found that both students' intrinsic motivation, which is defined as an internal desire to seek challenges and work to satisfy their curiosity and enjoy learning for learning's sake, and their extrinsic motivation, which is defined as motivation that is garnered through external rewards or punishments, declines as they progress from elementary school into secondary school

(Gottfried, Fleming, & Gottfried, 2001; Otis, Grouzer, & Pelletier, 2005; Ryan & Deci, 2000). In addition, there is also ample research that suggests that students' motivation to read their textbooks is low as well. McKenna, Kear, and Ellsworth (1995) note that while students have a positive attitude toward reading as first graders, this attitude decreases to indifference by Grade 6, and, according to Unrau and Schlackman (2006), as students move from sixth grade to eighth grade, their motivation to read continues to decline. However, Unrau and Schlackman tell us that if we can help students become intrinsically motivated, they will become more successful students, and Caine and Caine (2008) remind us that our minds do not work separately from our feelings and our commitment. We only learn when we have an intrinsic passion for what we are to learn. Self-efficacy, according to Vacca and Vacca (2008), also comes into play, since self-efficacy and motivation are interrelated. In other words, if students feel they can succeed in learning, they will, most likely, try to do their best.

How, then, can we best assure that our students gain such an intrinsic passion for learning and thus be motivated to learn? As noted earlier, "Adolescent learning involves interactive, purposeful, and meaningful engagement" (Crawford, 2007, p. 4). In other words, they must pay attention to what is to be learned, for, as Fisher and Frey (2008) inquire, "After all, if students aren't paying attention, how can they process new information?" (p. 34). Therefore, the first step to paying attention, and thus initiating the learning process, according to Fisher and Frey, is activating students' prior knowledge, a facet both Caine and Caine (2008) and Williams and Dunn (2008) have identified as a crucial element of the brain-compatible classroom. Vacca and Vacca (2008) agree and stress that the two most appropriate questions that students can ask are, "What do I need to know" and "How well do I already know it?" Such questions lead students to activate their prior knowledge by making predictions about what they will be studying and then setting purposes for themselves on how to accomplish that learning. Being able to make predictions and set purposes puts students on the path to regulating and monitoring their own learning, thus personalizing that learning. Furthermore, both Williams and Dunn (2008) and Oldfather and Dahl (1994) suggest that, since middle and high school students are essentially motivated by their own interests and desires to explore certain topics, in order to foster this motivation, teachers must provide a classroom that is response-centered, thus allowing students to think critically and make personal connections to what they are learning. In effect, the adolescent classroom must be one that moves away from teacher-directed instruction and employs, instead, student-centered learning, because, as stated above, student-centered learning leads to an intrinsic passion for all learning.

Thus, if students must pay attention in order to begin the learning process, what can teachers do to assure that their students do pay attention? According to Fisher and Frey (2008), students will pay attention when teachers invoke practices that elicit the students' curiosity, provoke them to contemplate questions about the material they are reading, and evoke information they have learned, all facets identified by Williams and Dunn (2008) as essential in the brain-compatible classroom. In effect, students must engage in anticipatory activities that provide a connection between what they already know about a topic or subject and the new material they will be learning. As Vacca and Vacca (2008) state, "They need to recognize how new material fits into the conceptual frameworks they already have" (p. 189). Finally, anticipatory activities should incorporate drama, humor, movement, emotion, puzzlement, doubt, surprise, perplexity, contradiction, and ambiguity into thought-provoking questions for students to ponder (Fisher and Frey; Vacca and Vacca). A discussion and examples of specific instructional strategies and activities to be used during the Entice the Learner stage of the block schedule lesson plan will be provided in this chapter.

STRATEGIES AND ACTIVITIES TO USE TO ENTICE THE LEARNER

Brain Writing

Brain Writing (Rodrigues, 1983), a variation of brainstorming, gives students an opportunity to share what they know about a subject without taking the risk of being wrong. Like any effective anticipatory activity, it encourages students to think about what they might already know about a topic to be studied, and the follow-up discussion it elicits helps to foster students' prior knowledge as well as engaging their interest in the subject to be studied.

Steps for Brain Writing

1. Provide students with a topic (word or concept) they will study or research.
2. Ask students to silently consider what they know or think they know about the topic and write the information down on a sheet of paper.
3. Next encourage students to share the written information in a small group. As students share and discuss their responses, have them record any additions, corrections, or comments in a different color ink.
4. Finally, invite the groups to share their knowledge and discuss what is known and what needs to be learned.

5. After all the groups have shared their information, students are ready to read, research, or listen to information to verify or refute the knowledge they shared.

See Figure 3.1 for an example of Brain Writing for social studies.

In addition to Brain Writing, several other variations to the brainstorming procedure exist and are especially effective for classes that achieve best when they operate in an active mode. While the basic procedures are the same, there are some changes in the process. Among the variations are Carousel Brainstorming (Silver, Strong, & Perini, 2001) and Exclusion Brainstorming (Blachowicz, 1991).

Example of Brain Writing for Social Studies

The Revolutionary War

1775
war of American independence
American revolution
colonists against Britain
13 colonies
Whigs
patriots
Tories
battles of Lexington and Concord
Continental Congress
slaves fought
Boston Tea Party
George Washington
Battle of Bunker Hill
Paul Revere
Valley Forge

Figure 3.1

Carousel Brainstorming

Carousel Brainstorming (Silver, Strong, & Perini, 2001) is a questioning technique that encourages students to develop and share their thoughts and ideas on a variety of questions. However, since sometimes students are reluctant to share what they know, or, in fact, they may not know very much about the topic, this strategy works to reduce their anxiety by allowing them to peruse a set of posted questions and choose ones that they feel they can answer comfortably. In addition, this strategy incorporates movement, one of the elements Fisher and Frey (2008) stress help students pay attention, and this movement around the classroom allows students to discuss their questions with their peers, a powerful vehicle for generating ideas. See Figure 3.2 for an example of Carousel Brainstorming for science.

Steps for Carousel Brainstorming

1. Prior to class, the teacher prepares a series of questions about a topic, word, or concept students will study or research and writes each question on a separate piece of chart paper. The pieces of chart paper are then hung up around the classroom or distributed to students at their desks or in their groups.

2. As students enter the classroom, the teacher distributes markers and asks students to read the various questions posted or placed at their tables and to write down all things they know about each question. (Note: If papers are distributed to the groups, ask each group to add their comments and then pass the paper to another group.)

3. When all the students have finished, the class can discuss the responses.

4. After the discussion, students are ready to read, research, or listen to information to verify or refute the knowledge they shared.

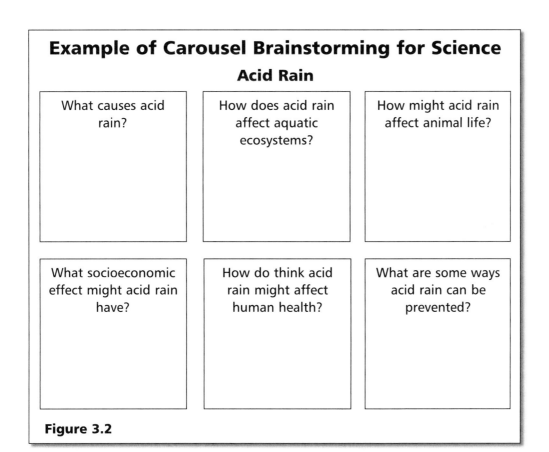

Example of Carousel Brainstorming for Science

Acid Rain

What causes acid rain?	How does acid rain affect aquatic ecosystems?	How might acid rain affect animal life?
What socioeconomic effect might acid rain have?	How do think acid rain might affect human health?	What are some ways acid rain can be prevented?

Figure 3.2

Exclusion Brainstorming

Brainstorming is an effective strategy for most students. However, in some instances students may encounter a concept or topic that they know relatively little about. In this case, students may benefit from yet another variation of brainstorming, Exclusion Brainstorming (Blachowicz, 1991). In exclusion brainstorming, the teacher writes the topic on the board and provides a list of words, some of which are related to the topic and others that are not. The power of this strategy lies in the discussion that transpires as students justify their responses for choosing or rejecting words.

Steps for Exclusion Brainstorming

1. Provide students with a topic, word, or concept they will study or research as well as a list of related and unrelated words.

2. Read the words with the students. Then, either individually, in small groups, or as a class, students determine which words are related to the topic and which are not related. Encourage students to justify and explain their choices.

3. After the discussion, students are ready to read, research, or listen to information to verify or refute the knowledge they shared.

4. As students read the assignment, they should notice whether the words in the Exclusion Brainstorming list are mentioned in the text.

See Figure 3.3 for an example of exclusion brainstorming for English/ language arts and Figure 3.4 for an example for mathematics.

Example of Exclusion Brainstorming for Language Arts/English

Nouns

person
shows action
place
common
proper
always capitalized
can be the subject of a sentence
collective
thing

Figure 3.3

**Example of Exclusion Brainstorming
for Mathematics**

Polygon

plane figure
open
segments
convex
concave
circle
irregular
endpoints
lines intersect anywhere
regular

Figure 3.4

Think-Pair-Share

An effective way to introduce a new topic, concept, idea, or issue or to transition into a continuation of the study of a topic previously introduced is the Think-Pair-Share strategy (Lyman, 1981). In this strategy, students simply pair up with another classmate and do any of the following:

a. Discuss a teacher-posed question about a new topic, concept, idea or issue.

b. Discuss a teacher-posed question to review the previous day's lesson.

c. Compare homework answers with each other and report their differences in answers.

Once students have completed their thinking, pairing, and sharing, they are ready to read, research, or learn about the topic.

A Variation on the Think-Pair-Share Strategy

A variation of the Think-Pair-Share strategy hinges on the final step of the process. After sharing with a single classmate, in this variation, the original pair shares their information with another pair, making a group of four, and then that group of four joins with yet another pair, so the final debriefing occurs in a group of eight students. As in the previous version, once students have completed their thinking, pairing, and sharing, they are ready to read, research, or learn more about the topic.

Give One–Get One

Give One–Get One (Silver, Strong, & Perini, 2001) is a strategy that helps develop or activate students' schema for a given topic by stimulating their background knowledge through social interaction among their community of learners. The Give One–Get One strategy can be incorporated into all content disciplines and used with various text genres.

Steps for Give One–Get One

1. The teacher formulates a topic related to the curriculum or text to be taught.
2. Students fold a piece of paper so it incorporates a select number of boxes (4, 6, 8, etc.) and number them accordingly.
3. Individually, students brainstorm their thoughts and ideas about the formulated topic and fill in the boxes in the first row of their paper.
4. Next, students circulate around the classroom and ask peers to add information by filling in the remaining row(s) of boxes with their thoughts and their names.
5. When all the boxes have been filled, students group together to share the thoughts and ideas recorded on their sheets by using such prompts as "John says . . . ; Sheila believes . . . ; Maria disagrees with. . . ."
6. The activity concludes with a whole class discussion as an introduction to the topic to be studied. See Figure 3.5 for an example of the Give One–Get One strategy.

Example for Give One–Get One for Science
Topic: Killer Whales

1. Jon They are big.	2. Jon They are so big, I believe they must eat thousands of pounds of food a day.	3. Jon They are warm-blooded.	4. Jon They live in oceans.
5. Sheryl I think they belong to the dolphin family.	6. Drew I think they have good vision so they can see small things in the ocean and eat them.	7. Melissa They use sonar to help get them around.	8. Emma I agree with Jon. They are warm-blooded, so they are mammals.
9. Tessa They are meat eaters.	10. Evelyn Sheryl says they belong to the dolphin family; they are probably pretty smart.	11. Kevin I think they eat everything, not just meat.	12. Arthur I disagree that they have good vision; their eyes are so tiny.

Figure 3.5

Three Step Interview

The Three Step Interview (Kagan, 1994) is a cooperative learning activity that helps students develop their listening skills while learning from the ideas and thinking of their classmates. Thus, it not only fosters students' prior knowledge, but it also allows them to make some predictions about what might appear in the text to be studied. Furthermore, since students work in groups as they follow the interview process, if they have little prior knowledge about the topic, they will gain information as they interview one another.

Steps for the Three Step Interview

1. First, the teacher develops an interview focus question. Possible focus questions might include the following:

    a. What do you know about this topic?
    b. What experiences have you had with the topic?
    c. Look at the cover of this book, the pictures, the table of contents, and the index. What do you think this book will be about?
    d. As you read the subheadings of the chapter, what do you think we will be learning about?
    e. What questions do you now have about this topic?

2. Next, students are paired off and placed in groups of four and given the interview question to ponder.

3. The first pair interviews each other while the second pair interviews each other.

4. When the pair interviews are complete, the pairs come together to form a circle, and all members of the group report out the information they gleaned from their partners.

5. As a final activity, the groups share their information with the entire class.

When the groups have discussed and compared their findings, they are ready to read or research the new topic they will study. See Figure 3.6 for a diagram and a set of questions for the Three Step Interview for biology.

Three Step Interview for Biology

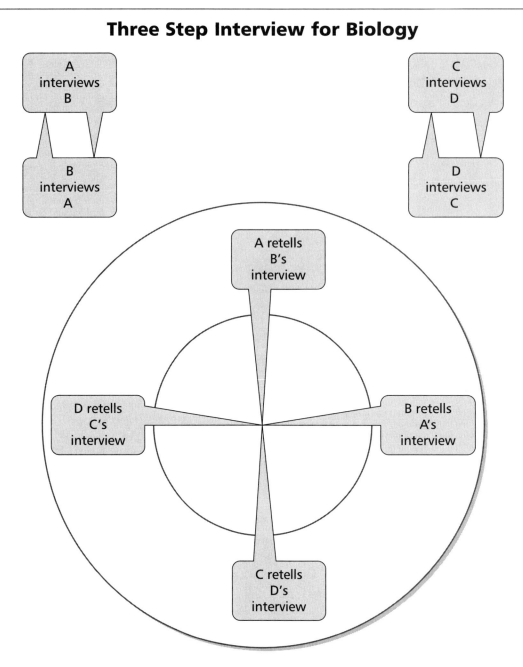

Questions for Three Step Interview for Biology

1. What do you know about biology?

2. Have you ever heard the word biology? Known anyone who took a biology class? What experiences have you had with biology? Explain.

3. Look at the cover of this book, the pictures, the table of contents, the index. What do you think this book will be about?

4. As you read the chapter subheadings, what do you think we will be learning about?

5. What questions do you now have about biology?

Figure 3.6

Hooks and Bridges

Hooks and Bridges (Silver, Strong, & Perini, 2001) is a strategy that asks students to think carefully and critically about a topic they will study or research by responding to a "hook" that will, in turn, become a "bridge" to learning. In effect, this strategy helps students gain a frame of reference for their learning, thus enabling them to recognize how the new material they are learning fits into the conceptual frameworks they already have, an ability Vacca and Vacca (2008) denote as an important technique in helping students focus their attention.

The hooks and bridges strategy revolves around a series of questions or hooks that are designed to grab students' attention. These are the following:

- **Mastery hooks** require students to share what they already know about the topic.

- **Understanding hooks** require students to examine the content or data and locate the basic underlying principles.

- **Self-expressive hooks** require students to use their imagination to respond to "what if" queries regarding the topic.

- **Interpersonal hooks** require students to use their own feelings and experiences to make a connection to the topic.

Once students have completed the Hooks and Bridges assignment, they are ready to see a relationship to the new material to be studied.

Steps for Hooks and Bridges

1. The teacher develops a set of hook questions that will generate student interest and focus their thinking. The hook questions should follow the pattern presented above.

2. The teacher asks students to respond to the questions individually, in small groups, or as a whole class and to complete the Hooks and Bridges graphic organizer.

3. When students have completed their responses, they can share and discuss them with the class.

4. At the completion of the discussion, the teacher creates a bridge by either asking a question or making a statement that helps students connect their responses to the new content or reading to be studied.

5. Finally, students are ready to read, research, or listen to information to verify or refute the knowledge they shared.

See Figure 3.7 for an example of Hooks and Bridges for science.

Example of Hooks and Bridges for Science

Mastery Hook	Interpersonal Hook
Hook: Think about what you already know about the solar system. What do you know about the sun and the planets that revolve around it? **Bridge:** Excellent! You seem to really know quite a bit about the solar system. Now let's see if the information we will now study will add on and perhaps make even clearer that information you already have.	**Hook:** Have you ever lain down and looked up at the sky during a dark and starry night? What did you see? Did you find any constellations? Did you see anything interesting? Did you know what you saw? How did it make you feel? **Bridge:** What fascinating things you saw and what interesting observations you made. Let's take time to study more about our solar system so the next time you gaze at the stars you will be able to spot and recognize even more phenomenal heavenly bodies.
Understanding Hook	**Self-Expressive Hook**
Hook: On August 24, 2006, Pluto was excluded from the list of real planets and termed a "dwarf" planet. Quickly skim the information on planets found on page 256 of your textbook. Why do you think Pluto was reclassified as a "dwarf" planet? **Bridge:** Great job! You are right on target about explaining why Pluto is really a dwarf planet. Next I will show you how we can locate some additional dwarf planets in our solar system.	**Hook:** Pretend you are the astronomer that was the first to recognize that Pluto was not a real planet. How would you share your new knowledge with other astronomers? How could you get them to believe your theories? **Bridge:** Good. Now let's take time to study some of the other great astronomical discoveries that have made an impact on our study of the solar system.

Figure 3.7

Mind's Eye

Reading researchers tell us that proficient readers visualize what they are reading; in effect they use their imagination to make pictures in their minds of the words in the text (Irvin, Buehl, and Radcliffe, 2007). As readers ourselves, we understand this concept well; it is probably why we usually prefer the book to any movie created on the basis of the book. It is this skill of visualizing that is at the crux of the Mind's Eye strategy (Brownlie & Silver, 1995, as described in Silver, Strong, & Perini, 2001), which plays upon students' curiosity and emotion by asking them to use their imaginations to create images in their minds as they listen to a series of key words chosen from the text to be read. This strategy not only helps students visualize the text they are to read but also to make predictions about it.

The strategy's process is begun as students listen to the key words and then attempt to visualize what they are hearing by making pictures in their minds. Ultimately they will produce a product to synthesize what they have heard by drawing a picture, asking a question, making a prediction about the text, or describing a feeling they have about the text.

Steps for Mind's Eye

1. First, select a section of an expository or narrative text and identify 20 to 30 terms or phrases that are essential to the meaning of the selection, listing them in the same order that they appear in the text.

2. Next, distribute a written list or read the words to the students and ask them to create a mental picture of each word, adding to that original image with each new word.

3. Once students have heard and created a mental picture of all the words, ask them to choose one of the following methods to share the mental picture they have created:

   a. Draw a picture of the story the words could make.

   b. Ask a question about the story the words could make.

   c. Make a prediction about the story the words could make.

   d. Describe a feeling they have about the story the words could make.

4. When students have completed their product, allow them to share it with the class and to compare and contrast the ideas they have about the story.

5. After they have all shared their products, ask them to reflect on the process and types of thinking they utilized in this assignment.

6. Finally, students are now ready to read, research, or listen to information to verify or refute the knowledge they shared.

See Figure 3.8 for an example of Mind's Eye for science and Figure 3.9 for an example for English/language arts. Figure 3.24 is a blackline master for this strategy.

Example of Mind's Eye for Science

Mind's Eye for Science

Directions: Listen to the following words and try to make a picture in your mind of what the words seem to tell you. Then, choose one of the following options to depict the image you get from the words.

Draw a picture   Ask a question   Make a prediction   Describe a feeling

blood → circulates → body → nutrients → oxygen → cells → tissues →
carries away waste → moves → circulatory system → vessels → arteries →
larger → smaller → veins → capillaries → moving → right side of the heart →
lungs → carbon dioxide → more oxygen → left side of the heart → circulates

Figure 3.8

Example of Mind's Eye for Language Arts/Literature

Mind's Eye for English : *To Build A Fire*

Directions: Listen to the following words and try to make a picture in your mind of what the words seem to tell you. Then, choose one of the following options to depict the image you get from the words.

Draw a picture   Ask a question   Make a prediction   Describe a feeling

cold gray day → Yukon trail → logger → snow → ice jams → 75 degrees below zero → big, native husky dog → jowls, muzzle, and eyelashes frosted over → ten miles to travel → creek → wet paws → frozen → numb fingers → matches → roaring fire → unexpected spring → falls through ice → wet to the knees → build a fire → snow covered spruce tree → snow falls on fire → panicked running → frozen hands → sacrifice dog → death → safety

Figure 3.9

Story Impressions

The Story Impressions strategy (McGinley & Denner, 1987) is similar to the Mind's Eye strategy. While this strategy is very effective with both exposition and narrative, it is especially successful when used with the plot line of narrative stories. In this strategy, as with the Mind's Eye strategy, students use clue words associated with important ideas and events in the content area or the plot line of the narrative to write their own version of the material prior to reading it.

This strategy asks readers to make predictions about the actual text they will read before they read, makes possible connections to that material, and helps improve their comprehension skills by providing them with fragments of the actual content. When students have composed their written version of the text based on the cue words provided, they are ready to compare their version to the actual text to be read, thus helping them make a connection between what they already know about a topic or subject and the new material they will be learning, so they can understand how the new material will fit into the conceptual frameworks they already have. Furthermore, since students must create their own possible version of the text they are to read, their curiosity to see the actual text, an element needed to generate student attention, is aroused.

Steps for Story Impressions

1. First, the teacher selects a section of an expository text or an essential section of a narrative text and identifies 10 to 12 terms or phrases that are essential to its meaning and lists them in the same order they appear in the text.

2. Next, the teacher distributes the words to the students and asks them, either individually or in small groups, to create a paragraph or a story that reflects their impression of what the text that these words come from might look like. In other words, they will use the words to create their own rendition of the text.

3. Students must use all of the words in the same order that they appear in the list.

4. When students have completed their writings and have shared them with the class, they are ready to compare their creation to the actual text. The teacher encourages them to modify, adapt, or revise their story based on what they have learned as a result of their reading.

See Figure 3.10 for an example of Story Impressions for social studies and Figure 3.11 for an example for English/language arts.
See Figure 3.25 for a blackline master for this strategy.

Example of Story Impression for Social Studies

Story Impressions for Social Studies French and Indian War: Use the words below to write a paragraph of your version of what the text might say.

France → England → 1754–1763 → Ohio Valley → General Braddock→ Indian allies → 1759 → James Wolfe→ Quebec, Canada → Montcalm → passage in cliff →British victory → Treaty of Paris

Figure 3.10

Example of Story Impression for Language Arts/Literature

Story Impressions for English: *The Black Cat*
Use the words below to write a paragraph of your
version of what the text might say.

moody man → black cat → alcohol → bite → knife → one-eyed
cat → wife → axe → cellar walls → police → howl

Once a very moody man had a black cat. He also had a serious problem with alcohol and was often drunk. One day he came home from work very drunk. As he walked into the house, the cat came running up and rubbed up against his leg. He got very mad at the interruption, and he kicked the cat, and it bit him. He got so mad that he grabbed a knife and cut the cat's eye out. His wife saw him hurt the cat, and she got really mad. She started screaming at him so he grabbed an axe and killed his wife and buried her and the cat in the walls of his cellar. Days went by, and pretty soon a neighbor reported the wife missing. When the police came to the man's house to ask about the missing wife, all they heard was a horrible howling coming from the cellar. It was the cat howling to be let out of the cellar walls!

Figure 3.11

Problematic Perspectives

Another strategy that makes use of the attention-getting elements of arousing students' curiosity, as well as asks them to utilize the conceptual frameworks they already have, is Problematic Perspectives (Vacca and Vacca, 2008). This strategy asks students to solve a problem from a specific perspective that relates in some way to the text to be read. For example, a student may assume the perspective of a soldier and German citizen during World War II, or an Iraqi woman under the Saddam Hussein regime, or a medical researcher during the Vioxx recall. The Problematic Perspectives strategy has its roots in the work of Pichert and Anderson (1977), which clarified that when students contemplate a problem from a particular perspective, their curiosity is aroused and they utilize the knowledge and experience they hold in their own conceptual framework to solve the problem they are presented. However, as Vacca and Vacca (2008) note, in order for the strategy to be successful, the teacher must provide adequate time for students to discuss the problem and seek an appropriate solution. Only when this is completed are students ready to study material related to the problem.

Steps for Problematic Perspectives

1. First, create a problematic situation that students will solve. The situation must include the key points of the topic to be studied, and the context of the problem should be defined as definitively as possible, so students clearly understand what they are to solve.

2. Then assemble students into cooperative learning groups and instruct them to generate as many possible solutions to the problem as they can.

3. When they have generated all the solutions they can, have them reach consensus as to which is the best or most promising solution, making sure that they can explain and justify their choice.

4. When they have made their final decision, instruct them to read the text related to the problem to validate the solution they posed. Encourage them to modify, adapt, or revise their solution based on what they learn as a result of their reading. See Figure 3.12 for an example of problematic perspective for social studies and Figure 3.13 for an example for English/language arts.

Example of Problematic Perspectives for Social Studies: Coming to America

Directions: In your group, read the following scenario and prepare a brief presentation of how you might solve the problem presented.

It is the late 1800s, and you are living in a European country that has suffered from crop failure, land and job shortages, rising taxes, and famine. Because you have heard that the United States is a land of economic opportunity and personal, political, and religious freedom, you leave your country and emigrate in search of a brighter future. You scrape up just enough money to travel across the sea in steerage as a third-class passenger. You arrive hungry, ill, tired, and broke. You know no one and cannot speak the language. Furthermore, you have landed at Ellis Island, in a city that is located on the sea, and you have always lived inland. What will you do? How will you communicate your plight? Learn the language? Where will you spend your first night? Get your first meal? Get health care? Move inland? Find a job? Get paid what you are worth? Be sure you are not taken advantage of?

Figure 3.12

Example of Problematic Perspectives for English/Language Arts (*A Light in the Forest* by Conrad Richter)

Directions: In your group, read the following scenario and prepare a brief presentation of how you might solve the problem presented.

It is 1754, and you, a British citizen living in the new land of America, have been taken hostage by a tribe of Indians as a replacement for the chief's son who was killed by your parents. You have lived with the Indian tribe as the chief's son now for 11 years. You are a free spirit, living in the forest and practicing the Indian ways and beliefs you have been raised with. Suddenly, the war has ended, and a treaty made between your Indian father's tribe and the government of your parents requires that you be returned to your British homestead. What is your first reaction to being returned to your rightful family? What differences between your old and new life do you see? How do you react to your new life? How do your parents react to you since you have lived for so many years with their enemies? What problems will you face? How will you handle the problems? What do you think will be your ultimate fate?

Figure 3.13

Character Quotes

Character Quotes (Blachowicz, 1993, as described in Buehl, 2001) is a strategy that acquaints students with a topic to be studied by examining the actual quotations of a character from a narrative text or of an actual person featured in an expository text. Students read these quotes and then generate thoughts about the character as a person, using the following questions:

- Who is talking to you?

- What can you tell about this person?

- What are some words that might describe this person?

- What words or phrases in the quote reveal what kind of person is speaking?

- What clues might hint at this person's identity? Age? Gender? Ethnic background? Income status?

- Is this person showing any emotion in this quote?

Steps for Character Quotes

1. First, the teacher selects a series of quotations that clearly reflect and illustrate the various elements of the character or the figure's personality.

2. Students then study the list of quotes and generate their impressions of the quotes using the questions presented above.

3. Working individually or in small groups, students consider the impressions they have gained from the quotes and generate a list of qualities and generalizations about the character.

4. The students then present their lists to the class.

5. After all the quotes have been discussed, the students develop a four- to five-sentence profile of the character.

6. As the students read the narrative or expository text from which the quotes came, they can add to their character's profile.

See Figure 3.14 for an example of Character Quotes for English/ language arts and Figure 3.15 for an example for social studies.

Example of Character Quotes for Language Arts (Dumbledore)

As much money and life as you could want! The two things most human beings would choose above all—the trouble is, humans do have a knack of choosing precisely those things that are worst for them.

Happiness can be found, even in the darkest of times, if one only remembers to turn on the light.

Curiosity is not a sin. . . . But we should exercise caution with our curiosity . . . yes, indeed.

Numbing the pain for a while will make it worse when you finally feel it.

You place too much importance . . . on the so-called purity of blood! You fail to recognize that it matters not what someone is born, but what they grow to be!

Time is making fools of us again.

Figure 3.14

Example of Character Quotes for Social Studies (Abraham Lincoln)

As I would not be a slave, so I would not be a master. This expresses my idea of democracy. Whatever differs from this, to the extent of the difference, is no democracy.

I am rather inclined to silence, and whether that be wise or not, it is at least more unusual nowadays to find a man who can hold his tongue than to find one who cannot.

Those who deny freedom to others, deserve it not for themselves; and, under a just God, can not long retain it.

Common looking people are the best in the world: that is the reason the Lord makes so many of them.

Stand with anybody that stands RIGHT. Stand with him while he is right and PART with him when he goes wrong.

Figure 3.15

Anticipation Guides

Anticipation Guides (Readence, Bean, & Baldwin, 2004) help students anticipate or make predictions about the content they will read by responding to a series of statements about that content. Anticipation Guides are valuable for several reasons. First, they act as a springboard for learning, since they ask students to consider the topic to be read before it is actually assigned, thus fostering prior knowledge. Second, they motivate students to read their assigned text, because the Anticipation Guide statements elicit students' curiosity by asking them to consider ambiguous statements that puzzle or surprise them, elements that both Fisher and Frey (2008) and Vacca and Vacca (2008) consider important in maintaining student attention. In addition, students become more interested in reading the assigned text because they are anxious to validate the predictions they have made. Furthermore, making predictions and then reading to confirm or reject them helps students set a purpose for reading. Finally, Readence, Bean, and Baldwin explain that since students make their responses prior to reading, they operate from their own experiences and belief systems, thus allowing them to respond with little fear of failure due to a lack of knowledge. In addition, due to their experiences and belief systems, they might hold preconceived misconceptions about some topics that negatively affect learning. This strategy helps alert teachers to these misconceptions and allows the teacher to modify the students' knowledge accordingly.

Steps for Using Anticipation Guides

1. Identify those major concepts or details in the selection that students should know or that may challenge or support their beliefs. Choose statements that stimulate student thinking and interest by presenting concepts about which they may have many opinions but few facts.

2. Next, give students time to respond to the statements (individually, in small groups, or in the whole group).

3. As each statement is discussed, ask students to justify or defend their opinions. Discourage yes or no responses. As an alternative, ask the class to come to a consensus.

4. Then, instruct students to read the selection to verify their predictions.

5. You may wish to include a column for prediction of the author's beliefs.

6. Finally, you have the option of using graphics instead of statements for the Anticipation Guide's content.

In effect, students locate sections in the text that support their newfound knowledge and record it in a graphic organizer. See Figure 3.16 for an example of an Anticipation Guide for English/language arts, Figure 3.17 for an example for mathematics, and Figure 3.18 for an example for social studies. In the Extended Anticipation Guide, which is discussed in detail in Chapter 5, students will revisit the Anticipation Guide and make changes to their predictions as a result of having read the selection.

Example of Anticipation Guide for English/Language Arts

Directions: In the column labeled *You,* place a checkmark on the line with any statement with which you tend to agree. Be prepared to support your opinions with examples.

After reading the novel *To Kill A Mockingbird*, by Harper Lee, compare your opinions with those expressed by the author through the events in the story, and check those statements that support the author's view in the column labeled *Harper Lee.*

	You	*Harper Lee*	*Statements*
1.	———	———	Children should be seen and not heard.
2.	———	———	Evil comes in many forms and may be hard to see.
3.	———	———	Sometimes children are wiser than adults.
4.	———	———	Courage means doing something even if it is difficult or frightening.
5.	———	———	We often fear what we do not know or understand.
6.	———	———	Older people always know what's best.
7.	———	———	All people are created equal.
8.	———	———	People who are different are to be avoided.
9.	———	———	Small towns can be dangerous places in which to live.
10.	———	———	Learning often occurs outside of the classroom.

Figure 3.16

Example of Anticipation Guide for Mathematics

Look carefully at the polygons below and predict their properties.

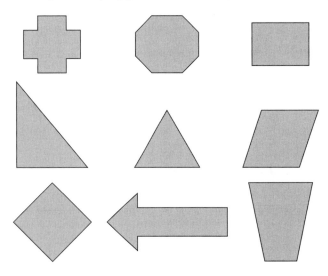

Figure 3.17

Example of Anticipation Guide for Social Studies
Anticipation Guide for "Children of the Holocaust"

Step 1: Read each statement below. In the column marked *You*, place a + by any statement you agree with and a − by any statement you disagree with.

Step 2: When you have completed Step 1, join with the other people (or one person at your table) and share your answers, justifying and defending your responses. When a consensus has been reached on whether a statement is true or false, record the appropriate mark in the *Group* column.

Step 3: When you have finished with your group responses, read the article entitled "The Children of the Holocaust" in the handout to find out what the author has to say. Record the author's responses in the *Author* column.

You	Group	Author	Statement
———	———	———	1. Jewish children were not the only children to suffer during the Holocaust. Gypsy children did too.
———	———	———	2. Early restrictions on Jewish children prohibited them from attending school.
———	———	———	3. Young infants and children up to the age of six were more likely to survive than older children.
———	———	———	4. Some Jewish children were given to Christian families for protection.
———	———	———	5. Over 100,000 children were hidden and thus protected from the Nazis.
———	———	———	6. Before the creation of concentration camps, some children were sterilized or even euthanized.
———	———	———	7. Children had a better chance of survival than adults did.
———	———	———	8. Older children were used as slave laborers.
———	———	———	9. Nine out of ten Jewish children were murdered during the Holocaust.
———	———	———	10. Approximately 1.5 million children died during the Holocaust.

Figure 3.18

True or False

A collaborative activity that intrigues students through the use of instant involvement and encourages them to learn about a topic is True or False (Silberman, 1996). This strategy encourages students to share their prior knowledge about a topic, issue, or concept they will study by responding to a series of true or false statements developed by the teacher. The statements are distributed to the students, and they circulate among their classmates questioning each other and discussing the statements to determine which are, in fact, true and which are false. As students seek to validate the veracity of the statements, they foster their own prior knowledge as well as that of their classmates. A variation of this strategy can be developed by asking students to respond to opinions rather than statements and then to discuss the opinion statements in an effort to reach a class consensus on each opinion.

Steps for True or False

1. Organize students into groups.

2. Compose a list of statements, half of which are true and half of which are false, that reflect the concepts of a topic, idea, or issue the class will study. Create as many statements as there are groups in the class, and write each one on a card.

3. Distribute one card to each group, and instruct students to circulate among their classmates to discuss the statements on their card in order to determine whether each statement is true or false. Encourage them to also use other sources in addition to the students in the class, such as books or the Internet, to validate the answers as well.

4. When all groups have determined the veracity of their statements, have each group present its findings to the whole class by first asking for a class opinion and then presenting their actual findings.

5. When all the groups have presented their findings, the class is ready to read or research the new topic they will study.

See Figure 3.19 for an example of the True or False strategy for science.

Example of True or False for Science

Directions: You will receive a card with a statement on it. It is your job to read the statement and then find out if it is true or false. You may use a variety of techniques to find out whether your statement is true or false, such as asking other students, surfing the Internet, looking in books, and so forth.

1. The loon spends the majority of its life on land, going in the water only to fish for food.
2. The loon chick is born with a full plumage, both down and feathers.
3. Many of the loon's bones are solid rather than hollow.
4. Loons are one of the oldest species of living birds, going back 50 million years.
5. Loons usually mate for life.
6. An overpopulation of loons seriously endangers the fish population of Canada.
7. Male loons do not incubate the eggs but only bring food to the female.
8. Loons communicate the hatching of their young to each other.
9. Loon chicks ride on the backs of their parents.
10. Loons can stay underwater for almost a minute at a time.
11. Acid rain endangers the loon population.
12. Loons usually give birth to six to seven babies.
13. The male and female loon look very different from each other.
14. Loons need lead to help digest their food.
15. The tourist trade benefits the loon population.

Figure 3.19

VOCABULARY STRATEGIES TO ENTICE THE LEARNER

Knowledge Rating

Knowledge Rating (Blachowicz, 1991) is a valuable strategy to utilize during the Entice the Learner phase for two reasons: It fosters prior knowledge about a topic to be studied while developing the students' vocabulary as well. The standard procedure for using Knowledge Rating asks the teacher to develop a list of vocabulary words or terms that are pertinent to the topic being studied and to share the list with the students prior to beginning their study of the topic. The words are listed in a grid format that asks students to determine their knowledge of each word according to the following categories: "can define," "have heard," "have seen," "can spell," "can say," and so forth. Once students have established their knowledge level for each word or term, they share their levels of expertise with the entire class.

Steps for Using a Knowledge Rating

1. Distribute a list of words or terms appropriate to the topic to be studied, with a grid of categories reflecting different amounts of knowledge of these terms.

2. Ask students to respond individually to each word or term by placing an X in the appropriate box on the grid. Students should be ready to explain or illustrate their responses. Possible categories in addition to those noted above might include "can give an example or an illustration," "can explain," or "can tell how I knew or learned the term."

3. After asking students to respond individually, encourage them to share their responses, first in small groups and then in a whole class discussion.

4. By encouraging students to share their responses freely during the whole class follow-up discussion, the teacher is able to ascertain which terms students know well and to foster students' prior knowledge of those terms with which they are unfamiliar.

See Figure 3.20 for an example of how to help your students evaluate their knowledge of mathematics vocabulary; see Figure 3.21 to see how they can evaluate their knowledge of English/language arts vocabulary terms, and see Figure 3.26 for a blackline master for this strategy.

Knowledge Rating for Mathematics

Word	Have Seen or Heard	Can Say	Can Define	Can Spell	Can Use in a Sentence	Can Give an Example	Don't Know at All
square root							
n							
negative square							
positive square							
perfect square							
radical expression							

Figure 3.20

Knowledge Rating for English/Language Arts

Word	Have Seen or Heard	Can Say	Can Define	Can Spell	Can Use in a Sentence	Can Give an Example	Don't Know at All
genre							
plot							
dénouement							
rising action							
falling action							
theme							
climax							
point of view							

Figure 3.21

Possible Sentences

Possible Sentences, created by Moore and Moore (1992), is another effective vocabulary strategy to utilize during the Entice the Learner phase, because it, like the Knowledge Rating strategy, not only develops the students' vocabulary but also fosters their prior knowledge of the topic of study. Utilized before the students begin reading, Possible Sentences asks students to make predictions about the meaning of the selection they will read based upon what they already know or can assume about the relationships among the words. They do this by combining the words to create a series of "possible sentences" about the selection to be read.

Steps for Possible Sentences

1. List 10 to 15 concept words that are essential to the understanding of the selection to be read. It is important to include a few words that are familiar to students as well as those that students do not know.

2. Next, ask students to choose two words from the list and write a sentence that they think might appear in the selection they will read.

3. Record the sentence, underlining the key words used, exactly as the students dictate it, even though it might not reflect an exact representation of the word's meaning or the text's content.

4. Continue this process until all the concept words have been used in sentences. If some words are completely unfamiliar to students, encourage them to guess at a meaning, reminding them that these are "possible sentences." (Note: Words may be utilized in more than once sentence as long as the new sentence presents a new concept.)

5. When all the sentences have been completed, instruct students to verify the authenticity of their sentences by reading the assigned selection. Buehl (2001) suggests that students evaluate each sentence by determining if

   a. the sentence is true because the text supports the prediction made in the sentence.
   b. the sentence is false because the text provides a different use of the terms.
   c. no decision can be made because the text does not clearly deal with the prediction made.

See Figure 3.22 for an example of Possible Sentences for mathematics and Figure 3.23 for an example for social studies.

Example of Possible Sentences for Mathematics: Mean, Median, Mode

Terms

mean   number   data   mode   value   often   median   mode   average
                  set

Possible Sentences:

1. The *mean* is the *average* of all the *numbers*.

2. The *mode* of a *data set* is the *number* used most *often*.

3. The *median* is the *number* that is the middle *value* in a *data set*.

Figure 3.22

Example of Possible Sentences for Social Studies: The Industrial Revolution

Terms

industrial   revolution   handmade   machines   textile   Britain
mechanized   cotton gin   machine-made

Possible Sentences:

1. *Handmade* products were replaced with *machine-made* products.
2. The *Industrial Revolution* began in *Britain*.
3. The *cotton gin* revolutionized the *textile* industry.
4. *Machines mechanized* the way products were created.
5. Products changed from *handmade* to *machine-made*.

Figure 3.23

CHAPTER SUMMARY

The first phase of the block schedule lesson plan format presented in this text, Entice the Learner, is designed to help the teacher prepare the students for what they are to learn. This phase, employing several of the brain-compatible facets identified by Williams and Dunn (2008), fosters the students' prior knowledge, helps to identify a purpose for their reading and learning, clarifies and teaches the vocabulary necessary for them to understand the concepts they will study, and, finally, arouses their interest in learning by helping them make predictions about and establish questions for the material that their studies will cover. This chapter provides a myriad of strategies. Some are simple to carry out, such as Brain Writing, Carousel Brainstorming, Exclusion Brainstorming, Think-Pair-Share and its variation, Give One–Get One, and the Three Step Interview. Others are more complex in nature and require that students make predictions, problem solve, and record their ideas in written form; these include Hooks and Bridges, the Mind's Eye, Story Impressions, Problematic Perspectives, Character Quotes, the Anticipation Guide, and True or False. Finally, Knowledge Rating and Possible Sentences facilitate vocabulary learning.

BLACKLINE MASTERS

Blackline masters for implementing the strategies in this chapter may be found on pages 98 through 100.

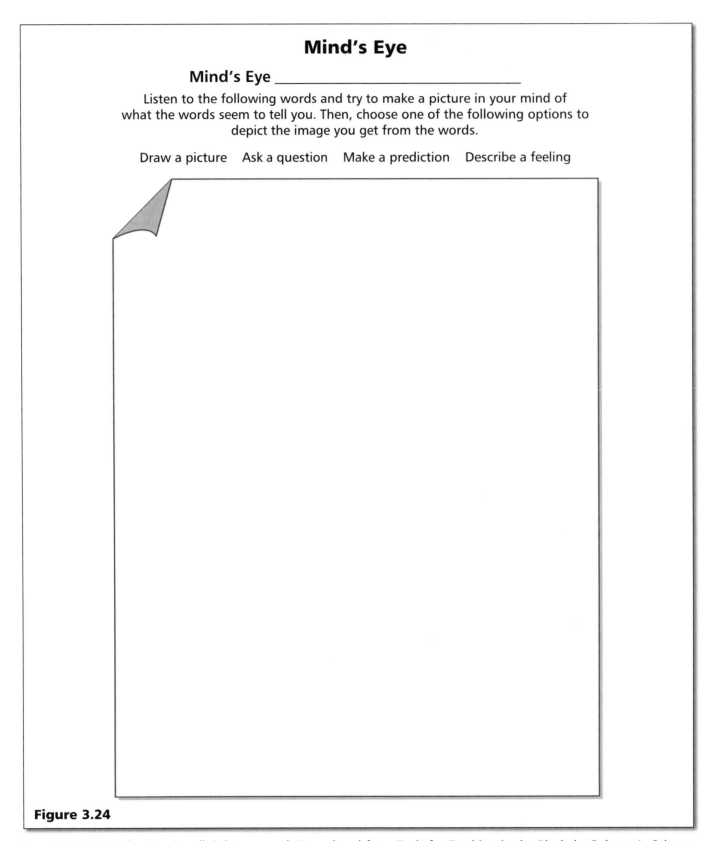

Mind's Eye

Mind's Eye _____

Listen to the following words and try to make a picture in your mind of what the words seem to tell you. Then, choose one of the following options to depict the image you get from the words.

Draw a picture   Ask a question   Make a prediction   Describe a feeling

Figure 3.24

Story Impressions

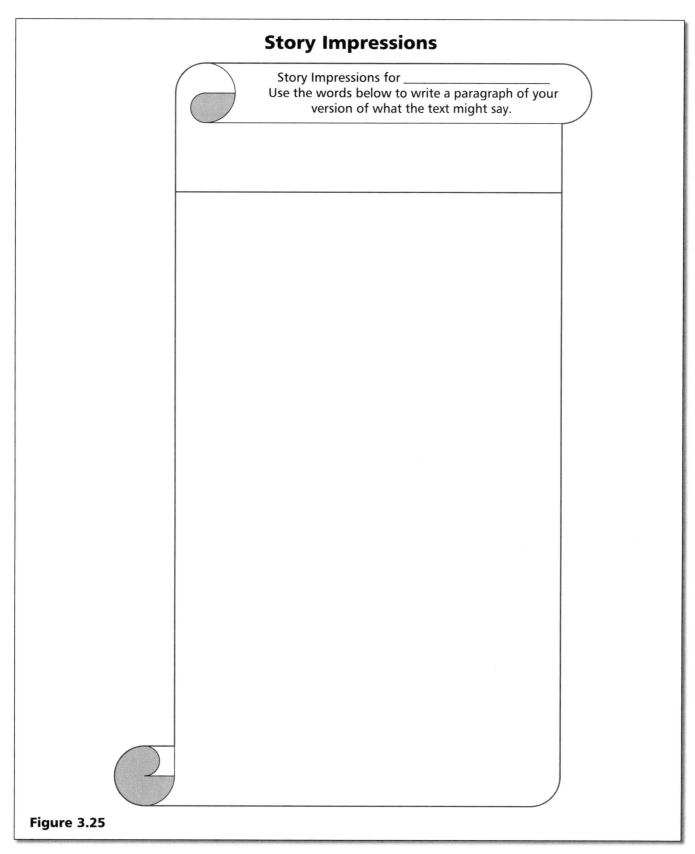

Story Impressions for _____
Use the words below to write a paragraph of your
version of what the text might say.

Figure 3.25

Knowledge Rating

Directions: In the space provided, write the words your teacher dictates. Respond individually to each category by placing a + in the appropriate boxes. Be ready to explain or illustrate your responses.

Word	Have Seen or Heard	Can Say	Can Define	Can Spell	Can Use in a Sentence	Can Give an Example	Don't Know at All

Figure 3.26

CHAPTER 4

*E*nlighten the Learner

The art of teaching is the art of assisting discovery.

—Mark Van Doren

THE SECOND PHASE: ENLIGHTENMENT

The second phase of an effective lesson plan for learning in the block, Enlighten the Learner, lasts approximately 15 to 20 minutes and is grounded in the facets of a brain-compatible classroom as outlined by Williams and Dunn (2008) and discussed in Chapter 2, specifically facets 1, 2, 4, 5, 7, and 8. The purpose of this phase is to focus on what the teacher can do to inform students so they can collect the information necessary to allow them proceed to the third phase of the block schedule lesson plan, where they will analyze, synthesize, categorize, and thus process that information. Therefore, in this, the second or Enlighten the Learner phase, teachers initiate a variety of learning opportunities such as direct instruction, teacher modeling, demonstrations, guest speakers, media presentations, and so forth to deliver the information to the students. This chapter will focus on specific instructional strategies and activities that can be employed during this second phase of the lesson plan format.

The Enlighten the Learner phase is probably the part of lesson planning that is most familiar to teachers, since it is the phase where we provide students with the information they must have in order to learn the concepts we have to teach. In effect, the most common way teachers usually handle this information-giving phase is to present a lecture, and, given the opportunity to teach in an extended period of 90 minutes, that lecture is often extended. In other words, a common occurrence is that given a longer time to teach, teachers often just talk longer. As a result, teachers sometimes find that their students fail to pay attention during these periods of lecturing.

Interestingly enough, however, Pat Wolfe (2001) tells us that "there is no such thing as not paying attention; the brain is always paying attention to something" (p. 81). Unfortunately, however, that something may not be an extended lecture, since, again in Wolfe's words, "Attention, as all of us know, is selective" (p. 81). Furthermore, Robert Sylwester (1995) reminds us that the brain is not built to pay attention for long periods of time. In fact, as a general rule, the attention span for young people is the same length as their chronological age in minutes plus or minus two. Therefore, according to Sousa (2006), a young adolescent has a 5- to 10-minute attention span while older adolescents have an attention span that lasts 10 to 20 minutes. Johnstone and Percival (1976) as cited in Middendorf and Kalish (1996) first illustrated that such a time format exists by studying students in over 90 lectures given by 12 different lecturers. They determined that the students' attention began to wane after 3 to 5 minutes and then began to fail at the 18-minute marker. Burns (1985) as cited in Middendorf and Kalish (1996) also investigated attention span during lectures by asking students to summarize what they heard in the lectures they attended. He found that students recalled the most information from the first 5 minutes of the presentations, and then their recall gradually dropped, reaching its lowest level after 15 to 20 minutes. Thus, it is not surprising that students enrolled in a classroom where an extended lecture format is followed may soon drift into a state of nonattentiveness.

And yet another explanation can be offered up to explain students' apparent inattentiveness. According to Savion and Middendorf (1994), the information transfer model that is at the core of the traditional lecture method fails to match what we now know about how humans learn. In effect, the brain does not just record information like some sort of a copy machine, but, rather, it synthesizes the information into meaningful chunks and then fits these into either an already formed schema or takes time to process the information and search for patterns in order to create a new schema. In effect, then, if the brain decides that the new information it is learning connects to information previously learned, the information takes on immediate meaning, but if no schema exists, the brain will create one. In other words, we learn by integrating new learning with whatever we already know about a concept—our old knowledge; this principle is supported by both Caine and Caine (2008) and Williams and Dunn (2008). Thus, in order to learn effectively from a lecture format, students need to make connections between what they already know and what they are learning, and this takes time for processing.

STRATEGIES AND ACTIVITIES TO USE TO ENLIGHTEN THE LEARNER

The strategies in this section, presented by Middendorf and Kalish (1996), allow teachers to present information in approximately 15 to 20 minutes, a time frame that is consistent with the amount of time students can easily stay attentive. The majority of these strategies are teacher-driven and will be familiar to most practicing educators; they include teacher modeling; teacher and student demonstrations, simulations, or laboratories; guest speakers; and small or whole group discussions as well as the two forms of Text Jigsawing, Reciprocal Questioning, and Socratic Seminars that are described in detail in Chapter 2. Other strategies are discussed in more detail below.

Direct Instruction of a Minilesson

According to Atwell (1987) and Calkins (1994), this strategy is an opportunity for teachers to teach focused lessons on the procedures, concepts, strategies, or skills students need to successfully comprehend their content area texts. For example, students can be taught how to use the dictionary, how to successfully complete a graphic organizer to learn new vocabulary, how to use an index or table of contents in a text, how to take effective notes utilizing a note-taking strategy such as About/Point, a strategy discussed in Chapter 5, and how to successfully utilize reading strategies like predicting, visualizing, or making connections to self, text, or world. For best results, teachers should follow specific steps in conducting a minilesson. These are the following:

1. Introduce the procedure, concept, strategy, or skill that is the focus of the minilesson.

2. Demonstrate the procedure, concept, strategy, or skill by modeling specific examples for students to see.

3. Provide both an opportunity and adequate time for students to practice the procedure, concept, strategy, or skill.

4. Next, as students utilize what they have learned, monitor and evaluate their progress, offering reinforcement and encouragement as needed.

5. Finally, after students have successfully internalized the procedure, concept, strategy, or skill, ask them to reflect on how they will make use of their new knowledge in their future learning, thus initiating the transfer of knowledge to new situations.

Audio Presentations/ Videotapes/CD-ROM Presentations

Middendorf (1993), as cited in Middendorf and Kalish (1996), suggests using a brief selection from a media source to inform students and provides the following guidelines to make the clip most effective. First, teachers should not feel committed to showing the entire run of the media source selected. Instead, they should use those portions that are most significant or relevant to the topic being studied and that will thus make the best use of the time allotted to this phase of the lesson. Second, before the media clip is presented to the students, the teacher should introduce the clip by providing an overview of it and explaining how it relates to the topic to be studied and why it is necessary for students to know about the topic. In addition, specific questions that relate to the media clip should be introduced to the students to provide a purpose for their learning. Next, during viewing or listening, the teacher should stop the media presentation at appropriate times, so students can discuss what they have seen or heard and ask questions.

Interactive Lectures

There are several strategies that can keep students involved while they are listening to a lecture or watching a media presentation. These strategies can be used intermittently during the lecture or video at crucial moments determined by the teacher. The strategies are the following:

1. **Say Something:** Harste, Woodward, and Burke (1984) suggest that if, after listening to a lecture, watching a video, or even reading a section of text, students are given the opportunity to stop and talk about what they have heard, seen, or read, their understanding or comprehension will improve because they will have the opportunity to clarify any misconceptions they have as well as share their reactions. In effect, knowing that they will discuss their learning shortly after it is presented will encourage them to remain focused during this Enlighten the Learner phase of instruction. Steps for the Say Something strategy are as follows:
   a. Group students into pairs.
   b. Then, after they have listened to, viewed, or read the assignment, ask them to stop and talk to their partners to share a comment or a question about the assignment.

   c. This process may be repeated at various intervals depending upon the length of the assignment.

2. **Write a Question:** In this strategy, the students are instructed to write down one to three questions that relate to the material presented to them during the text jigsaw process, the minilesson presented, or the lecturette provided. While this strategy is not particularly new, since we often ask students if they have any questions, Middendorf and Kalish (1996) tell us that the act of actually writing down the questions empowers students and gives them the confidence to ask the questions.

3. **Press Conference:** This strategy, from Thiagarajan (1988) as cited in Middendorf and Kalish (1996), mimics the Write a Question strategy discussed above, but this time students focus on trying to generate questions that might be asked at a press conference that detail the topic being studied.

4. **Exam Questions:** To utilize this strategy from Angelo and Cross (1993) as cited in Middendorf and Kalish (1996), the teacher asks students to consider the examination formats they often encounter in class—such as multiple-choice, short-answer, true or false, and essay questions—and then, in small groups, generate a set of questions that might appear on such an examination. The questions are then shared with the class, which is asked to critique them and then offer possible answers. For specific practice with essay questions, teachers can utilize the PORPE strategy (Simpson, 1986). This five step strategy helps students (P) predict essay questions that the teacher might ask; (O) organize the key ideas needed to answer the essay question and state them in their own words; (R) rehearse the key ideas that were organized in the O step of the strategy; (P) practice writing the answer to the essay question; and finally (E) have the answer evaluated either by classmates or through a self-evaluation. Specific steps for the PORPE strategy follow:

   a. PREDICT: Based on a review of the material learned, students predict what essay questions they think the teacher might ask. (Note: for this step to be successful, students must understand the basic terminology utilized in test questioning. See Figure 4.1 for a list of common essay terms and definitions.)

Common Essay Terminology and Definitions

Comment	Discuss the topic/issue briefly.
Compare	Cite both similarities and differences in two or more topics/issues.
Contrast	Stress differences in two or more topics/issues.
Criticize	Discuss both the positive and negative sides of a topic/issue.
Define	Express a clear, concise meaning for a term.
Demonstrate	Provide your opinion, evaluation, and judgment about a topic/issue.
Describe	Relate the topic/issue in sequence or story form.
Diagram	Organize information about a topic/issue and its parts and relationships through a flowchart, a chart, or some other graphic presentation.
Differentiate	Clearly show how two topics/issues are different.
Discuss	Explore and examine, in an organized fashion, a topic/issue from all sides.
Distinguish	Show the difference between the main points of two topics/issues.
Enumerate	Present the main points of a topic/issue in a numbered list or outline form.
Evaluate	Present a value judgment that focuses on the negative and/or positive worth of a topic/issue; be sure to state evidence for your opinion.
Explain	Clearly present a discussion, emphasizing cause-effect relationships, to interpret or analyze a topic/issue.
Illustrate	Use a picture, diagram, or graphic aid to present specific examples of a topic/issue.
Interpret	Explain or show a specific application of a given topic/issue.
Justify	Determine why a position or point of view regarding a topic/issue is right.
List	Similar to the term *enumerate,* but requires a formal numbering or a formal outline.
Outline	Present a set of facts or ideas by listing the main and subordinate points in a formal outline.
Prove	Use evidence to present the facts about a topic/issue in a clear, logical argument.
Relate	Show how two or more topics/issues are connected to one another.
Review	Summarize the major points, facts, principles, ideas, similar results, or similar characteristics of a topic/issue.
Show	List, in order of occurrence, importance, or logic, the key points about a topic/issue.
Solve	Support any concept or idea with specific facts and proof.
State	Present a brief statement of a position, fact, or point of view or examples about a topic/issue.
Summarize	Briefly present the main points relevant to an issue/topic; eliminate details.
Support	Clearly provide facts and proof for any statements made regarding a topic/issue.
Trace	Present sequentially how a series of facts about a topic/issue are related in terms of time, order, or cause and effect.

Figure 4.1

b. ORGANIZE: Next, students synthesize and summarize the main points needed to answer the essay question and organize them by using either an outline or a graphic organizer.

c. REHEARSE: Students then use the outlines or graphic organizers they have created to orally recite the answer to the essay question, complete with specific examples to support their ideas. This recitation will help transfer the answer into their long-term memory.

d. PRACTICE: Next, students write their response to the essay question. At this point, the teacher might suggest they jot down the outline or graphic organizer they used in the REHEARSE step in the margin of their paper. The teacher should also remind them to rephrase the original essay question as a part of their written response and to use transition words to help their ideas flow along logically.

e. EVALUATE: Finally, when students have finished writing their responses, they are ready to evaluate them. Students may evaluate their own or work in small groups where students evaluate each other's responses. In order to facilitate an effective evaluation of the responses, students should check them for accuracy by revisiting the text or comparing their answers with a checklist provided by the teacher.

5. **Concrete Images:** In this strategy from Frederick (1981) as cited in Middendorf and Kalish (1996), after students have listened to the lecturette, text jigsaw, demonstration, simulation, or laboratory, they are asked to reflect on what was heard and then state a concrete image of a scene, event, moment, or fact that impacted them. These concrete images are then listed on the board, and, as students review them, they focus on identifying themes or patterns or filling in missing points from the information presented to them.

6. **Picture Making:** Similar to the Concrete Images strategy discussed above, the Picture Making strategy (Berquist and Phillips, 1975, as cited in Middendorf and Kalish, 1996) encourages students to visualize the principles or questions that emanate from the information provided to them during this phase of the lesson. In small groups, students discuss their visualizations and then create an illustration of one on chart paper. Each visualization is then shared with the class through explanation and discussion.

Both the Concrete Images and Picture Making strategies discussed above are similar to the Mind's Eye strategy (Brownlie & Silver, 1995, as described in Silver, Strong, & Perini, 2001), discussed in detail in Chapter 3.

Paired Discussions

Wright (1994), as cited in Middendorf and Kalish (1996), provides a strategy that not only helps students focus on the discussion, but also fosters their problem-solving abilities. In this strategy, students pair with a partner and, for three to four minutes, discuss a question or a problem that relates to the topic of the lecture. They may analyze, synthesize, or evaluate what they have heard, or react to a theory, concept, or information presented in the lecture.

Send a Problem

This strategy, developed by Wright (1994) as cited in Middendorf and Kalish (1996), asks students to compose a question that relates or reviews the gist of the lecture information and write it on an index card. The card is then passed to a fellow student who, in turn, writes his or her version of an answer and then passes it on to another student. When all the cards have been returned to their original source student, the questions are shared and discussed with the entire class.

Learning Centers/Learning Stations

While we tend to identify Learning Centers with elementary school learning, they can also be effectively used in middle and high school as well. At these levels, it is probably more prudent to label such centers, which are designated for learning a specific activity, as learning stations rather than learning centers. Ideally, learning station activities last between 15 and 20 minutes and engage students in developing a particular skill or learning about a specific topic or concept. Students can be sent, individually or in groups, to the various learning stations according to the teacher's objectives for the activities as well as the dynamics of the students in the class. Above all, using Learning Stations is an effective strategy simply because it engages students in active, on-task learning. They are not required to sit stone still and listen to a lecture, but, instead, are free to move about from task to task and participate in hands-on activities.

Learning Stations can be designed to accompany any of the disciplines taught in a middle and high school curriculum and can be used to reinforce, enrich, or review instruction. For example, in some classrooms, general stations, such as a vocabulary station, a student reflection station, a paired teaching station, a graphic organizer station, a visualize it/draw it station, or an independent reading station, might be created. In other classrooms, stations may be more curriculum-based, such as in science, where the stations might include hypothesis creation, experimentation, data collection, recording, and analysis; or in social studies, where the stations might reflect map study, culture, language, important events, famous people, or research; or in mathematics, where the stations might include math facts, calculator and graphing calculator practice, word problems, and problem solving. In addition, the many actvities that can be developed for learning stations can be used in all of the stages of the block schedule lesson plan format. While a myriad of possibilities for Learning Stations exist, it is not the purpose of this book to provide detailed instructions on how to create such effective Learning Stations. However, we can provide one example of an effective Learning Station adapted from the work of Sonja Boekenhauer, Ericka Smith, and Megan Thomas, science teachers at Carpentersville Middle School, Carpentersville, Illinois, who developed these stations to help their students understand the concepts of animal and plant cells.

Example: Learning Stations for the Study of Cells in Biology

Learning Station 1: Let's Question—
Using the Verbal/Linguistic Intelligence

This station utilizes the verebal/linguistic intelligence to help students process the information they have learned about the cells. After listening to a lecture, reading a passage from the text, or viewing a video or CD about cells, students go to this station to develop Question-Answer Relationships (QARs; see Chapter 2 for a detailed example of the QAR strategy). Here are the directions to students that accompany this station:

1. Review pages 38 to 45 in the text or your notes from the lecture or video/CD.

2. In your group, create four QARs for this section. On one piece of paper, write all four questions, labeling each by type. Place your questions in the red folder at the station.

3. On a separate piece of paper, write the answers to your questions; place the answers in the green folder at the station.

4. When you have completed your questions and answers, select a set of questions that have been developed by students from other science classes from the blue folder and answer them. Place your completed answers in the yellow folder at the station.

Learning Station 2: Everybody Looks—
Using the Visual/Spatial Intelligence

In this station, students utilize the visual/spatial intelligence to study both a plant cell and an animal cell under a microscope and then recreate the images they have seen, coloring and labeling them appropriately. The directions to students that accompany this station are:

To study a plant cell:

1. Individually, choose a leaf from the collection of leaves at the station.
2. Place the leaf under the microscope and locate a plant cell.
3. Sketch a picture of the plant cell, coloring it appropriately.
4. Label the various parts of the cell that you can see.

To study an animal cell:

1. Use a toothpick from the supply at the station and gently rub it against the inside of your cheek to secure a sample of the cheek's membrane.
2. Gently place the residue from the toothpick on the glass slide provided.
3. Place the slide under the microscope and locate an animal cell.
4. Sketch a picture of the animal cell, coloring it appropriately.
5. Label the various parts of the cell that you can see.

Learning Station 3: Look Like a Cell—Using the Bodily/Kinesthetic and Interpersonal Intelligences

This station utilizes the bodily/kinesthetic intelligence to help students recall the different parts of the cell and their functions by connecting them to a movement they create. Then, working together as a group, the students utilize the interpersonal intelligence to create a cell in movement. The directions to students that accompany this station are as follows:

With the members of your group, you are going to use movement to create either a plant or an animal cell.

1. From the beaker at the station, choose one slip of paper.
2. Open the slip of paper to learn what cell part you have been assigned.
3. According to the cell part you have drawn, perform the appropriate movement described below:
   a. Nucleus—brain of the cell: Point to your brain.
   b. Cell membrane—allows things to move in and out of the cell: Walk forward and backward.
   c. Cell wall—protects the cell: Put your hands up and pretend to be a wall.

     d. Cell mitochondria—powerhouse of the cell: Show your muscles.

     e. Chloroplasts—foodmakers of the cell: Walk and rub your belly.

     f. Cytoplasm—jelly-like substance: Wiggle your fingers.

4. Once your group has assembled, perform your assigned actions together to create a "moving cell."

As a concluding activity, the students can stage a whole class presentation of a moving cell.

Learning Station 4: Show Me a Cell—Using the
Visual/Spatial and the Logical/Mathematical Intelligences

In this station, students utilize a combination of the visual/spatial intelligence and the logical/mathematical intelligence to creater a foldable booklet that synthesizes their knowledge of the two types of cells through a compare/contrast list. The directions to students that accompany this station are as follows:

1. Fold a piece of paper in three sections to make a trifold pamphlet.

2. On the front section of the outside of the pamphlet, create a title for your pamphlet.

3. For the middle section of the outside of the pamphlet, think about what you have learned about animal and plant cells and write your responses to the following:

     a. ***Reflection:*** What did this lesson about animal and plant cells teach me?

     b. ***Connection:*** How does this lesson apply to my life?

     c. ***Perfection:*** In what other ways could I learn this lesson?

4. On the back section of the outside of the pamphlet, write your name, your class period, your teacher's name, and the date.

5. On the inside section of the first flap, draw and label a detailed picture of a plant cell.

6. On the inside section of the third flap, draw and label a detailed picture of an animal cell.

7. In the center section of the inside, develop a Venn Diagram illustrating the similarities and differences between plant and animal cells.

See Figure 4.2 for a diagram of the pamphlet.

Example of Cell Learning Station 4

Outside of the Pamphlet

Cover title	Reflection: Connection: Perfection:	Student's name Class period Teacher Date

Inside of the Pamphlet

Drawing of plant cell with appropriate labels	Venn diagram of similarities and differences between an animal and plant cell	Drawing of animal cell with appropriate labels

Figure 4.2

CHAPTER SUMMARY

This chapter has focused on the second phase of an effective lesson plan format for the block schedule. The activities described for this second phase take into account several of the facets identified by Williams and Dunn (2008) as necessary for a brain-compatible classroom. In essence, the chapter suggests a variety of ways teachers can inform students so the students can collect the information necessary to allow them to proceed to the third phase of the lesson plan format, Engage the Learner. Specific strategies and activities presented in this chapter are considered in two categories. The first is teacher-centered strategies such as teacher modeling; teacher and student demonstrations, simulations, and laboratories, with a reference to the Text Jigsaw strategy; a guest speaker; audio presentations/videotapes/CD-ROM presentations; and direct instruction of a minilesson. The second is teacher-student interactive strategies; these include Say Something, Write a Question, Press Conference, Exam Question, Concrete Images, and Picture Making as well as small or whole group discussions, Reciprocal Questioning, Socratic Seminar, Paired Discussions, Send a Problem, and, finally, Learning Centers/Learning Stations.

CHAPTER 5

Engage the Learner

Tell me and I forget. Show me and I remember. Involve me and I understand.

—Chinese proverb

THE THIRD PHASE: ENGAGEMENT

In the previous chapter, the second phase of the lesson plan format, Enlighten the Learner was discussed. This phase provided a variety of strategies that enable students to smoothly move into the third phase of an effective lesson for learning in the block, Engage the Learner. The Engage the Learner phase lasts approximately 20 to 30 minutes; is grounded in the facets of a brain-compatible classroom as outlined by Williams and Dunn (2008) and discussed in Chapter 2, specifically facets 1, 2, 3, 4, 5, 7, 8, and 9; and focuses on how students analyze, synthesize, categorize, and thus process the information they gathered during the previous two phases of the lesson plan. In sum, as students participate in the Engage the Learner phase, they become active learners by validating predictions they made, keeping their purpose for learning in mind, and self-monitoring their understanding as they complete a variety of activities that cause them to interact with their text. In addition, during this phase students make connections between what they are learning (new knowledge) and what they already know (old knowledge) by utilizing instructional frameworks for monitoring and guiding their learning, such as study guides and graphic organizers created or provided by the teacher to help them accomplish these tasks efficiently. This chapter will focus on the specific instructional strategies and activities that can be employed during this phase of the lesson plan format.

As discussed above, during the Engage the Learner phase, students are encouraged to be active and engaged in their learning. In effect, they must become strategic readers. Roe, Stoodt-Hill, and Burns (2007) tell us that strategic readers

> actively interact with the text and the context (reading task and purpose); they connect information in the text with preexisting knowledge. They have a repertoire of strategies and know how to use these strategies to comprehend. Strategic readers stop to reflect on what they have read. (p. 128)

Furthermore, Paris, Lipson, and Wixson (1983) remind us that strategic readers are readers who are in control of their reading because they move through a series of steps in the reading process: declarative knowledge, procedural knowledge, and conditional knowledge. First, strategic readers utilize their declarative knowledge to understand what is involved in the reading they must do. They realize they must make meaning or sense of what they are reading, and, as a result, they analyze the reading task before them by determining whether the text is narrative or expository and then set a purpose for their reading and establish a reading goal to be accomplished (Paris, Wasik, & Turner, 1991). Next, they use their procedural knowledge to help determine how to approach and carry out the reading task they have set for themselves. In effect, strategic readers initiate a plan of action to achieve the goals and purpose they have set by choosing the strategies they will use as they read. For example, they might choose to first read the questions at the end of the chapter to see what they will be required to know; then skim the introduction and summary sections of the text in order to gain an overview of the concept to be learned, and, finally, read the chapter carefully while taking notes. Finally, strategic readers make use of their conditional knowledge, the knowledge that alerts them when a particular strategy is working and when it is not working and should be abandoned for another strategy. In sum, strategic readers monitor and regulate their comprehension, recognize that they are understanding what they are reading, and, when they realize that their understanding is failing, they know what to do to repair or "fix up" their lack of understanding, whether that is to reread a passage, look up an unfamiliar vocabulary word, or ask a teacher for help. By the same token, if their comprehension is progressing well, they may skip sections that contain irrelevant or extraneous details or skim over a passage that contains familiar material. As a result, they have metacognitive awareness and control over the reading process and their learning activities (Baker & Brown, 1984; Royer, Cisero, & Carlo, 1993).

Given that we can identify the characteristics strategic readers possess, what can we, as educators, do to help our students become strategic readers and thus strategic learners? First, we need to provide our students with extensive opportunities to read for a variety of purposes. Second, they must be taught how and given opportunities to make and confirm predictions, visualize, summarize, draw inferences, generate questions, and make connections. They need to learn to synthesize information from various sources, analyze and evaluate authors' ideas and perspectives, and make applications to authentic situations, all the while monitoring their own understanding. In addition, they must recognize how a text is organized and maintain and utilize a system for organized note taking. Finally, they need to be able to read and understand the graphical representations located in their texts such as tables, charts, maps, and graphs (Moore, Bean, Birdyshaw, & Rycik, 1999).

While the following sections will provide a series of strategies that will equip students to become strategic learners, we first need to understand how to best help students effectively learn these strategies. Peterson, Caverly, Nicholson, O'Neal, and Cusenbary (2000) note that for students to effectively learn a strategic approach to reading and learning, they must be taught how, why, and when to use each strategy. Furthermore, Winograd and Hare (1988) have determined that five critical elements are needed to guide the direct explanation of all strategies:

1. First, the processes of the strategies must be carefully explained, so they are meaningful and sensible to the students.

2. Next, students must be made aware of the direct benefits of the strategies and why they need to learn them.

3. Then, students must be given a step-by-step explanation of how the strategies work.

4. Next, students must learn exactly in and under what circumstances the strategies they are learning are most effective.

5. Finally, the students must take time to reflect on how well the strategies work for them.

In addition to adhering to the process described above, teachers must also utilize the gradual release of responsibility model developed by Pearson and Gallagher (1983) as a way of helping students acquire the strategies that will help them become strategic learners. This process begins with the teacher demonstrating and modeling the steps of a strategy using an actual piece of text. Next, in pairs or small groups and with teacher support, students practice the strategy. Finally, when students become proficient in the use of the strategy with teacher and/or peer support, they are ready to use the strategy independently. To effectively teach comprehension strategies, Roe, Stoodt-Hill, and Burns (2007) have developed a plan of action that is outlined below.

1. First, the teacher engages the students by motivating them, activating their interest, and fostering their prior knowledge. Once the students' attention has been captured, the teacher introduces the strategy, names it, and explains how and why students will find it is valuable for learning.

2. Second, the teacher must model the strategy for the students using, as Roe, Stoodt-Hill, and Burns (2007) suggest, a "think-aloud," wherein the teacher verbalizes how the strategy is being used in the reading of the text.

3. Next, the students practice the strategy themselves until they can comfortably apply it independently. (Note: In my experience, this guided practice usually needs to be done several times. Doing the strategy a single time does not usually result in a full understanding of how the strategy can be used efficiently.)

4. Finally, once students can independently utilize the strategy correctly, the teacher can release all learning to the student.

Given the processes detailed above, it is important that, as teachers introduce the various strategies discussed in this book, they follow the suggestions provided by Winograd and Hare and Pearson and Gallagher so that students not only learn the strategy but understand why and when they should use the strategy.

STRATEGIES AND ACTIVITIES TO USE TO ENGAGE THE LEARNER

There are a myriad of strategies that students can efficiently use during this phase. Several of these strategies such as Reciprocal Teaching, Question-Answer Relationship (QAR) Strategy, Questioning the Author, ReQuest, Socratic Questioning, Structured Note Taking, and Learning Stations were discussed in previous chapters. Additional strategies are discussed below. To help guide teachers in which strategies to utilize, these strategies have been categorized according to how they might be best used by students to facilitate their learning.

STRATEGIES FOR MONITORING THE READING

Doug Buehl (2001) reminds us that a leading difference between proficient and struggling readers is that proficient readers carry on an internal monologue while they read. This internal monologue is often referred to as metacognition, or thinking about thinking. In effect, it is metacognition that allows readers to be aware of what they are doing throughout the reading process and how successful what they are doing is. Vaughan and Estes (1986) have developed two strategies, INSERT and SMART, that are designed to assist students in using metacognition to help them interact with the text they are reading and to monitor their understanding of it.

SMART

SMART, the Self-Monitoring Approach to Reading and Thinking (Vaughan & Estes, 1986), fosters students' ability to concentrate on how their reading is progressing. Basically, like the INSERT strategy discussed below, it requires that students, as they read, determine what they actually understand and what they do not understand and then presents them with some fix-up strategies to help them persist through the reading until they are able to make full sense of what they have read.

Steps for SMART

1. Assign students a chunk of text to read.
2. As they read, instruct them to lightly mark a ✓ in pencil next to each paragraph that they clearly understand and to mark a ? next to any paragraph that contains material that they do not understand.
3. When students reach the end of the chunk of material, ask them to retell, in their own words, what they have read. Encourage them to look back at the text to help them report out.
4. Next ask students to concentrate on the paragraphs they have marked with a ? and engage in any of the following fix-up strategies:
   a. Reread the difficult paragraph in an effort to make sense of it.
   b. Isolate the problem by trying to determine exactly why the paragraph is difficult to understand by considering whether the paragraph contains
      1. a difficult, unfamiliar vocabulary word?
      2. difficult or confusing language? an unfamiliar subject?

    c. Attempt a fix-up strategy.

        1. Look up the vocabulary word in the glossary or dictionary.

        2. Look over other parts of the chapter such as the introduction, summary, chapter questions, pictures, or other graphics.

    d. Try to focus on exactly what you do not understand or what confuses you.

    e. Ask the teacher for help.

See Figure 5.1 for an example of SMART for science.

Example of SMART for Science

√ Loons have stout bodies, long necks, pointed bills, and three-toed webbed feet, and they spend most of their time afloat. The common loon in summer is very striking with its black-and-white checkered back, glossy black head, and characteristic white necklace around the throat. The white feathers of the belly and wing linings are present year-round, but all loons have grayish feathers in the winter. Immature loons resemble adults in winter plumage. √ Males and females look the same, although males are generally larger. Loon √ adults are large-bodied, weighing from 2.7 to over 6.3 kilograms and ? measuring almost a meter from bill tip to outstretched feet. Their bill, which is black in color, is quite large, averaging 75 millimeters in length. ?

? The skeleton and muscular system of a loon are designed for swimming and diving since their legs are placed far back on their body, allowing for excellent movement in water but making them ungainly on land. Their heads can be held directly in line with their necks during diving to reduce drag, and their legs have powerful muscles for swimming. Many bones of the loon's body are solid, rather than hollow like those of other birds. These heavy bones make loons less buoyant and help them to dive. The loon's large webbed feet provide propulsion underwater, with the wings being used underwater only for turning. √

Retelling: These paragraphs describe the color and size of the common loon. They are black and white, and the male and female look alike. They spend most of their lives in water and are good divers because they have solid bones. Their large webbed feet help too.

Fix-up Strategies: I can't picture exactly how big they are because I do not understand what kilograms and millimeters are. I don't know what *ungainly* means either, so that sentence confuses me.

Figure 5.1

INSERT

INSERT (Interactive Notation System to Effective Reading and Thinking) (Vaughan & Estes, 1986) asks students to "insert" their own thoughts into the text as they are reading by determining (a) whether or not they understand what they are reading, (b) whether or not they have encountered new or important ideas, (c) whether or not they agree with what they have read, and (d) what they might be wondering about. As Sturtevant and Linek (2004) tell us, since the determinations made by the students are "conscious and noted, they can be discussed, examined, justified, and modified. These types of decisions provide a basis for critical thinking and reasoning by clarifying what one thinks about the ideas presented in the text" (p. 138).

Steps for INSERT

1. Introduce students to the notations they can make during reading. Sturtevant and Linek (2004) suggest the following marks to indicate the decisions made, but teachers and students can design their own notations if they wish:

    a. I agree = ✓ (The statements confirm what you already knew about the topic.)

    b. I disagree = X (The statements contradict what you already knew about the topic.)

    c. That's new = + (The statements provide information that is entirely new relative to what you already knew about the topic.)

    d. That's important = ! (You realize the statements provide important information about the topic.)

    e. I wonder = ? (The statements lead you to do more thinking about the topic.)

    f. I don't understand = ?? (The statement confuses you.)

2. Notations can be made directly in the text, if students are allowed to write in their texts.

3. If students are not allowed to write in their texts, they can

    a. cover the text with a plastic transparency and write their notations in the appropriate places.

    b. put the notations on sticky notes and attach them to the text in the appropriate places.

4. For struggling learners, Sturtevant and Linek (2004) suggest that the strategy be introduced slowly, perhaps having students utilize only the ✓ and the X notations at first.

See Figure 5.2 for an example of INSERT for social studies.

To help students effectively utilize the SMART and INSERT strategies, it is imperative that the teacher model each strategy out loud using an overhead transparency to show possible markings before allowing students to complete them independently.

Example of INSERT for Social Studies

√ When Adolf Hitler rose to power in 1933, the quality of life in Germany was very poor. Unemployment was high, and, as a result of World War I, Germany was in a depression. It was Hitler's promise to improve the quality of life for Germany that made him a popular choice as a ruler. Once in power, he convinced the German people that one "race" alone, the Jewish people, was responsible for the problems, and, under the Nazi regime, he set out to cure Germany, and other countries such as Poland, Italy, and Russia, of "The Jewish Problem." ??

EARLY RESTRICTIONS

As a result, Jews and their children suffered, and the world of Jewish children under the Nazis rapidly changed. First, Gentile children were taught that Jewish and Gypsy children were racially inferior, and by 1935, even their closest friends avoided the Jewish and Gypsy children, sometimes becoming   + hostile, unfriendly, and even spiteful. In April 1933 one of the first laws that affected Jewish students, the "Law against Overcrowding in German Schools and Universities," was enacted. It established that the number of Jewish   + children in schools was not to exceed 1.5 percent of the total number of students. At first, Jewish children of war veterans and those with a non-Jewish parent were exempted, but on November 15, 1938, all German Jewish and Gypsy children were prohibited from attending German schools.   !
! While they were assigned to segregated Jewish schools, by July 1942 these were all closed. Suddenly the world of childhood and adolescence, usually a time of happiness and growth, became a world of shrinking horizons and ?? vulnerabilities. Jewish and Gypsy children could no longer belong to the same clubs and social organizations as Gentile children and were even banned from using public recreational facilities and playgrounds.

Figure 5.2

STRATEGIES FOR GUIDING THE READING

As teachers, we know that in some instances our students are faced with text books that are difficult for them to read, because they lack the prior knowledge needed to understand the concepts presented, because the information in the texts may not be explained as fully as students need, or even because the readability of the text is too difficult for the them. Furthermore, another daunting task that often faces students is how to best determine what facts are important to remember and which are not. Can you remember the first time you used a highlighter to underline important information in your reading? I remember that my page was completely yellow; I had underlined everything! Students usually have this same problem, because they begin underlining, highlighting, or note taking as soon as they start reading rather than processing what they have read first, determining the importance of what they have read, and then beginning the highlighting or note-taking process.

Another situation that complicates the learning process for students is the amount of reading they are assigned. Too often teachers will simply ask students to read the entire chapter rather than asking them to read the text in chunks. However, for some students, especially those who lack the appropriate level of prior knowledge needed to understand the concepts presented or have a reading level that is not commensurate with the readability of the text, this makes the reading task complex and difficult. Furthermore, as Williams and Dunn (2008) remind us, one way to help students process what they read, and thus help facilitate their learning, is to ask them to read their assignments in chunks and then process what they have read in a variety of ways. In addition, although most students are familiar with study guides, many of them fail to use them as they were intended to be used, that is, as a vehicle to help them understand instructional reading materials. In fact, most of us have stories to relate about students who merely look at a question in the guide, skim the text for the answer, write it down, and move on to the next question. Needless to say, such practice does not do much to help students understand what they are studying. In order to facilitate this understanding, students need to make use of strategies that will guide their reading effectively. The following strategies offer specific ways to help students through this processing task.

Guided Note Taking

Guided Note Taking is an effective way to introduce students, who are novices at the process of note taking, to a method of identifying important facts and details in any assignment they are given. In essence, this strategy provides a structured framework, or template, of the critical ideas in a reading assignment, lecture, or video with blanks where important points exist, so that students can fill in these blanks as they read or listen or watch the video. Heward (1994) suggests that Guided Note Taking increases the likelihood that students will engage in and respond to lesson content because the guided notes help students distinguish between relevant and irrelevant content.

Steps for Guided Note Taking

1. Choose a segment of text, lecture, or video, and determine the important facts and details students must glean from the assignment.

2. Prepare, in paragraph form, a handout that outlines the order of the main ideas and critical details in the assignment with blank spaces provided so that students can fill them in.

3. To effectively introduce this strategy, the teacher should model the process using an overhead transparency and filling in the appropriate blanks.

See Figure 5.3 for an example of Guided Note Taking for social studies and Figure 5.4 for an example for science.

Example of Guided Note Taking for Social Studies

When _____ _____ composed our _____, he created a document that has survived, despite many tests, for over _____ _____. This document has been proclaimed as an example of _____ not only by the _____ _____ but many other nations around the world as well.
    The _____ _____ of the _____ contained _____ articles that outlined the _____ of _____ as well as the _____ between _____ and a process to _____ it. As it was being _____, two states, _____ and _____ became concerned over how the _____ of the _____ would be protected. To assure that these states would _____ the _____, the writers included the _____ of _____, which are the first ____ _____. These _____ guaranteed that people have the rights of _____, _____, _____, _____, _____, _____.

Figure 5.3

Example of Guided Note Taking for Science

I. The principles of genetics were established in _____ by _____ _____.

II. Mendel performed his experiments using the _____ _____.

A. Mendel began by studying two types of seeds _____ and _____.

   1. When he planted a _____ seed it grew into a _____ plant.

   2. When he planted a _____ seed, it grew into a _____ plant.

   3. The _____ generation of _____ and _____ plants were called the _____ generation or _____.

B. Mendel's second experiment crossed a _____ plant and a _____ plant.

   1. This type of cross planting is called _____.

   2. In a _____ cross, the plant differs by _____ trait, the _____ _____.

C. The _____ of the _____ generation is called the ___ _____ or _____.

   1. All of the _____ generation's seeds were _____.

   2. That means that the _____ trait was _____ and the _____ was _____.

D. In a third experiment, Mendel _____ the plants from the _____ generation to _____.

   1. In the _____ generation, most of the seeds were _____, but a few were _____.

   2. A count showed that _____ of the seeds were _____ and _____ of the seeds were _____.

Figure 5.4

Reader's Questions

As in Guided Note Taking, the Reader's Questions strategy (Sejnost & Thiese, 2007) provides a framework for helping students identify the main points from the text they are reading. As students read, they record their responses to the reader's questions, WHO, WHAT, WHEN, WHERE, WHY, and HOW in a graphic organizer chart. The value of this strategy lies in the fact that to complete the answers, students may need to reread parts of the text, thus fostering their ability to comprehend, organize information, stimulate thinking, and make connections to the content being studied. In addition, the graphic organizer also serves as a memory tool to be used in class discussions.

See Figure 5.17 at the end of the chapter for a blackline master to use with this strategy.

Steps for The Reader's Questions

1. Create a graphic organizer that includes the following Reader's Questions. (Note the responses in parentheses are merely suggestions.)

    a. Who? (person or topic)

    b. When? (did the person or topic live, travel, become successful, occur?)

    c. Where? (did the person live, travel, or become successful? did the subject or topic occur?)

    d. What? (were the person's or topic's beliefs, problems, adventures, failures, ideas? did events occur?)

    e. How? (were problems solved, relations made, recognition achieved?)

    f. Why? (was the person or topic important?)

See Figure 5.5 for an example of Reader's Questions for social studies or science and Figure 5.6 for an example for music appreciation.

Example of Reader's Questions for Social Studies or Science

Directions: As you read about the topic assigned, complete the graphic organizer by providing information to answer the following questions:

1. Who or what is the topic? If it is a person, name the person and list key people in his or her life. If it is a topic, name significant people associated with the topic.

2. When and where did the topic take place? Or, when and where did the person live, travel, and become a success?

3. What were the person's beliefs? Or, what were the topic's main elements?

4. How did the person relate to others? Solve problems? Achieve recognition? Or, how did the topic become recognized, successful?

5. Why was the person or topic important?

Who or What: Sputnik

When and Where: (Time and Place)	What: (Beliefs or Elements)	What: (Problems)	How: (Solutions, Recognition)	Why: (Was the Topic, Person Important)
• October 4, 1957 • Russia launched Sputnik I • November 3, 1957, Soviet Union launched Sputnik II manned with a dog, Laika	• artificial satellite launched during high cycle of solar activity • launched new political, military, technological, and scientific, developments • caught world's attention	• led to U.S. fear that Soviet Union would launch nuclear weapons on the world • U.S. public was furious that U.S. was becoming a second to the U.S.S.R. in technology	• U.S. scraps Vanguard Project begun in 1955 • Werner von Braun begins work on Explorer project • January 31, 1958, Explorer I launched	• marked beginning of the space age and the U.S. and U.S.S.R. space race • Sputnik led to the creation of the National Aeronautics and Space Act which created NASA on October 1, 1958

Figure 5.5

Example of Reader's Questions for Music Appreciation

Directions: As you read about the topic assigned, complete the graphic organizer by providing information to answer the following questions:

1. Who or what is the topic? If it is a person, name the person and list key people in his or her life. If it is a topic, name significant people associated with the topic.

2. When and where did the topic take place? Or, when and where did the person live, travel, and become a success?

3. What were the person's beliefs? Or, what were the topic's main elements?

4. How did the person relate to others? Solve problems? Achieve recognition? Or, how did the topic become recognized, successful?

5. Why was the person or topic important?

Who or What: Mozart

When and Where: (Time and Place)	What: (Beliefs or Elements)	What: (Problems)	How: (Solutions, Recognition)	Why: (Was the Topic, Person Important)
• born January 27, 1756, in Salzburg, Austria • died in 1781 at age 35	• child prodigy • charming personality • daring: copied a forbidden piece of papal music • loved to improvise • desired public recognition • adhered to Italian, Austrian, and German traditions in his music	• his music fell out of favor • poor financial decisions • lavish lifestyle led to poverty • unhappy marriage • ill wife	• moved to less expensive homes • worked as a court composer	• musical genius • master of fugue and counterpoint • great writer of melodies • brought Viennese classical style to its height • composed over 600 works

Figure 5.6

5W Model

The 5W Model (Bellanca & Fogarty, 2003) can be termed an abbreviated adaptation of the Reader's Questions strategy, since it employs a similar format. See Figure 5.7 for an example of the 5W Model for social studies or science and Figure 5.18 at the end of the chapter for a blackline master for the strategy.

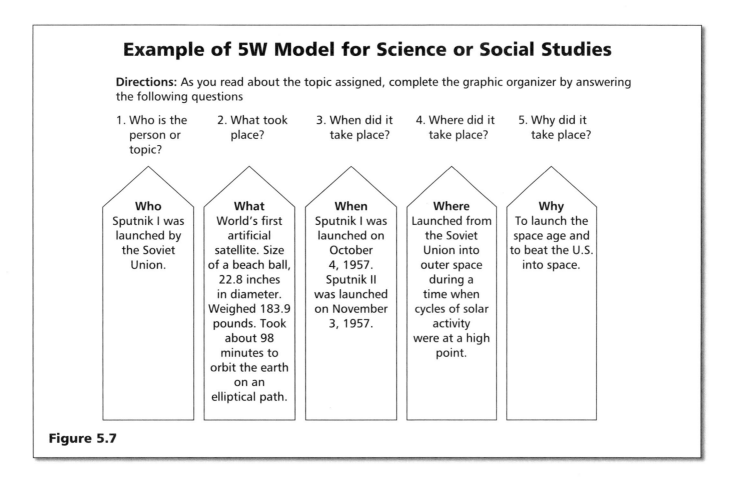

Example of 5W Model for Science or Social Studies

Directions: As you read about the topic assigned, complete the graphic organizer by answering the following questions

1. Who is the person or topic?	2. What took place?	3. When did it take place?	4. Where did it take place?	5. Why did it take place?
Who Sputnik I was launched by the Soviet Union.	**What** World's first artificial satellite. Size of a beach ball, 22.8 inches in diameter. Weighed 183.9 pounds. Took about 98 minutes to orbit the earth on an elliptical path.	**When** Sputnik I was launched on October 4, 1957. Sputnik II was launched on November 3, 1957.	**Where** Launched from the Soviet Union into outer space during a time when cycles of solar activity were at a high point.	**Why** To launch the space age and to beat the U.S. into space.

Figure 5.7

Extended Anticipation Guide

Yet another strategy to help students determine the importance of the concepts they read is the Extended Anticipation Guide, an outgrowth of the Anticipation Guide developed by Readence, Bean, and Baldwin (2004). As discussed in Chapter 3, the Anticipation Guide helps students anticipate or make predictions about the content they will read by responding to a series of statements about that content. This extension, developed by Duffelmeyer, Baum, and Merkley (1987), encourages active involvement during reading by asking students to carefully reread the text to locate the textual support that validates their predictions about the statements, and, if no textual support is found, students write, in their own words, exactly what the text reveals about the concept presented in the statement. The most effective way to utilize the Extended Anticipation Guide with students is to first develop a regular Anticipation Guide (see Chapter 3) and label it Part I, and then develop a graphic organizer in which students can enter the information they locate as they reread to validate their original prediction and label it Part II. See Figure 5.8 for an example of an Extended Anticipation Guide for Social Studies.

Example of Extended Anticipation Guide for Social Studies

Extended Anticipation Guide for "Children of the Holocaust"

Step 1: Read each statement in Part I and place a + by any statement you agree with and a – by any statement you disagree with.

Step 2: Next, read the article "Children of the Holocaust." If the text supports your choice for each statement in Part I, place a check in the *Support* column in Part II below. If the text does not support your choice, place a check in the *No Support* column and write what the text does say in your own words.

Part I

Response   *Statement*

_____   1. Both Jewish and Gypsy children suffered during the Holocaust.

_____   2. Early restrictions on Jewish children prohibited them from attending school.

_____   3. Children younger than age six were more likely to survive than older children.

_____   4. Some Jewish children were given to Christian families for protection.

_____   5. Over 100,000 children were hidden and thus protected from the Nazis.

_____   6. Before the creation of concentration camps, some children were sterilized or even euthanized.

_____   7. Children had a better chance of survival than adults did.

_____   8. Older children were used as slave laborers.

_____   9. Nine out of ten Jewish children were murdered during the Holocaust.

_____   10. Approximately 1.5 million children died during the Holocaust.

Part II.

	Support	No Support	In Your Own Words
1.			
2.			
3.			
4.			
5.			
6.			
7.			
8.			
9.			
10.			

Figure 5.8

About/Point

The About/Point strategy, developed by Morgan, Meeks, Schollaert, and Paul (1986), is another strategy that fosters students' ability to identify the main idea and supporting details found in the texts they read. To use the strategy, readers locate the subject of the text and state it succinctly, and then they enumerate the points made about that topic. See Figure 5.9 for an example of About/Point for mathematics and Figure 5.10 for an example for science. Figure 5.19 at the end of the chapter presents a blackline master to use with this strategy

Steps for About/Point

1. Provide students with a short expository or persuasive text.

2. Distribute the About/Point graphic organizer, and model how to use it using the following steps:

    a. Read a section of text to determine the main idea or point and write it in the POINT section of the graphic organizer.

    b. Next, reread the text to identify one to seven (no more than seven, since seven is the number of concepts the brain remembers efficiently) details to support the main point, and record them in the ABOUT POINT section of the graphic organizer.

3. Distribute another short text and have students read the text individually or with partners and complete an About/Point organizer.

Example of About/Point for Mathematics

Directions: Read the assigned passage, and write a sentence that tells what the passage was about, its MAIN IDEA. Next, list up to seven points that support or tell more about the main idea.

This reading is about the properties of a parallelogram.

And the points that support it are as follows:

1. Opposite sides are equal.

2 Opposite sides are parallel.

3. Opposite angles are equal.

4. Diagonals bisect each other.

5. Same side interior angles are supplementary.

6. It forms two congruent triangles.

Figure 5.9

Example of About/Point for Science

Directions: Read the assigned passage and write a sentence that tells what the passage was about, its MAIN IDEA. Next, list up to seven points that support or tell more about the main idea.

This reading is about whales.

And the points that support it are as follows:

1. There are over 70 kinds of whales.

2. They range in size from 4 feet to 100 feet.

3. Whales are mammals.

4. Whales take in air through their blowholes.

5. Whales travel as far as 5,000 miles as they migrate in the winter.

6. They live in groups or pods.

7. Whales communicate through high- and low-pitched sounds and whistles.

Figure 5.10

Magnet Summaries

Writing summaries is one way of helping students crystallize what they have read into its main points. In summary writing, students first read and comprehend, and then, finally, restate what they have read in their own words. An effective summarizing strategy that asks students to process their reading chunk by chuck is the Magnet Summaries strategy (Buehl, 2001). In this strategy, students read a passage from the text, identify a key word from it, choose additional words or phrases that are related or attracted to the key word (hence the word MAGNET), and then weave this all into a summary of the passage. Once all the sections of the reading assignment have been completed, students develop a full-blown summary of the entire assignment.

Steps for Magnet Summaries

1. Assign students a passage to read. The best method is to begin by assigning the text developed under a single subheading section.

2. Once the students have read the passage, ask them to choose a key word that is related to the concept being discussed. It is important to make students understand that this key word is like a magnet in that it attracts the information in the passage that is important to the topic.

3. Next, have students recall all the details from the passage that are connected to the magnet word, and record these on an index card.

4. After the magnet word and the supporting details have been recorded, have students weave them into a short summary of no more than one to two sentences.

5. This process should be repeated until all sections of the assigned reading have been read.

6. When all chunks of the assignment have been summarized, students should arrange their summary sentences in logical order and develop a coherent summary for the entire reading assignment. Be sure that students edit and revise their sentences so their summaries flow smoothly.

There are several advantages to teaching students how to summarize using the Magnet Summaries strategy. First, it provides students with a logical and simple procedure for determining relevant and irrelevant details as they synthesize the information they have read. Second, it introduces students to the process of chunking and processing the materials they are asked to read. While this strategy appears simple, its success depends on teacher modeling to guide students through the process before they produce Magnet Summaries independently. See Figure 5.11 for an example of a Magnet Summary for mathematics and Figure 5.12 for an example for science. Figure 5.20 at the end of the chapter presents a blackline master for the strategy.

Example of Magnet Summary for Mathematics

KEYWORDS

quadrilateral   congruent   parallel   angles

MAGNET WORD
trapezoid

KEYWORDS

isosceles   base congruent   supplementary   four

SUMMARY

A trapezoid is a *quadrilateral* that has *four* sides, one of which is *parallel* to another one *and two angles which are supplementary*. An *isosceles* trapezoid has both *congruent base angles* and *congruent* non *parallel* opposite sides.

Figure 5.11

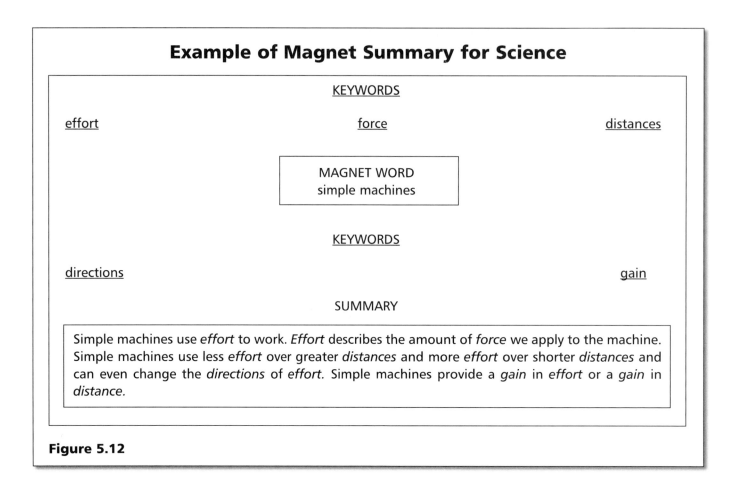

Example of Magnet Summary for Science

KEYWORDS

effort   force   distances

MAGNET WORD
simple machines

KEYWORDS

directions   gain

SUMMARY

Simple machines use *effort* to work. *Effort* describes the amount of *force* we apply to the machine. Simple machines use less *effort* over greater *distances* and more *effort* over shorter *distances* and can even change the *directions* of effort. Simple machines provide a *gain* in effort or a *gain* in distance.

Figure 5.12

Sketch to Stretch

The Sketch to Stretch strategy (Harste, Short, & Burke, 1988) is an effective method that helps students monitor their comprehension, strengthen their listening skills, and improve their ability to visualize or image what they are reading. In effect, students read a chunk or section of text, visualize a picture of what it says in their minds, and then create an image to represent those ideas. To accomplish this, the teacher reads a section of text to the students and then asks them to draw a sketch of what they have heard. To help students clarify their understanding of what they have heard, the teacher can distribute copies of the text for students to read and use to revise their drawings and thus clarify details or expand on the meaning. When students have completed their drawings, they share them with a partner and discuss what they have drawn, focusing on what details are important to remember from the text. They then record their details in the summary of important details section of the graphic organizer.

Steps for Sketch to Stretch

1. Choose a section of text to read to students.

2. Explain that they should listen carefully while you read and try to visualize what they hear by making a picture in their minds.

3. Distribute the Sketch to Stretch graphic organizer.

4. Read one section of the selection aloud and ask students to sketch what they have visualized in the first box of the organizer.

5. After students complete their sketch, distribute copies of the text for students to read and advise them to revise their drawings by adding any details they have gleaned from reading the text.

6. When their drawings are complete, ask students to pair off and talk about their sketches, explaining why they drew what they did. Tell pairs to come to a consensus on what is important to remember from the text they listened to and read.

7. Finally, tell students to summarize these important facts in the second box next to the picture.

8. This sequence should be repeated until students can proceed on their own to complete the reading selection with adequate understanding.

See Figure 5.21 at the end of the chapter for a blackline master of this strategy.

Jot Charts

Jot Charts, as discussed in Vacca and Vacca (2008), help students make sense of what they have read by providing a matrix to help them organize information according to how the concepts are alike or different. In effect, by utilizing Jot Charts, students can gather, organize, and synthesize the data they have collected from a variety of sources such as readings, lectures, videos, and so forth into a two dimensional matrix with topics, categories, or items recorded horizontally and specific questions or characteristics recorded vertically. Jot Charts can be used in any content area and can be developed in a variety of ways.

Steps for Jot Charts

1. Analyze the content students will study to identify areas that can be compared and contrasted.

2. Develop a matrix that illustrates the similarities and differences evident in the content in the following way:

   a. List the topics, categories, or items to be analyzed or described across the top of the matrix.

b. List the specific questions or characteristics areas that can be compared or contrasted down the side of the matrix.

3. Distribute the matrix, and instruct students to complete it by jotting down information they have collected in the appropriate sections of the matrix.

See Figure 5.13 for an example of a Jot Chart for science or for classes in foods or health.

Example of Jot Chart for Science, Foods, or Health

Type of Organic Compound	Composed of	Characteristics of	Role It Plays	Examples
fats	composed of carbon, oxygen, hydrogen atoms (COH)	won't dissolve in water and/or is repelled from water	provides the body with stored energy	butter, corn oil, ham, peanuts, wax
carbohydrates	composed of carbon, oxygen, hydrogen atoms (COH)	three main types: monosaccharides, disaccharides, and polysaccharides	major source of food and major source of quick energy for the body	rice, beans, pasta, corn, potatoes
nucleic acids	two different, distinct, but related chemical forms: deoxyribonucleic acid (DNA) and ribonucleic acid (RNA)	stores all the heredity information of all organisms on earth	master information-carrying molecule for the cell	polymers
proteins	composed of carbon, oxygen, hydrogen atoms (COH) and nitrogen and amino acids	large molecular weight (10,000–1,000,000)	basic building blocks of cell and cell structure and of hair, nails, muscles, and connective tissue like tendons, cartilage	peanuts, eggs, beans, fish

Figure 5.13

Pyramid Diagram

The Pyramid Diagram (Solon, 1980) is another strategy that not only helps students recognize which concepts and details are important to remember about a topic but also helps them process those facts and details as they draw conclusions about the materials and, finally, create a well-developed summary of what was read.

Steps for Pyramid Diagram

1. Assign a text segment for students to read.
2. Develop a question for students to focus on as they read the assigned material.
3. Next, as students read, ask them to record on index cards all the information they find pertinent to the focusing question. Instruct them to place only one fact on each index card. This will become Layer 4 in the Pyramid Diagram.
4. Once students have completed their reading and recording, group them in pairs or small groups and instruct them to collaborate to combine all the recorded information and then brainstorm possible categories under which the facts could be organized. Once they have chosen the categories they wish to use, instruct students to write each category title on an index card. This will become Layer 3 in the Pyramid Diagram.
5. Next, students should sort their fact cards under the appropriate category card.
6. When all the facts have been categorized, ask students to develop a title that reflects the overall topic. This will become Layer 1 in the Pyramid Diagram.
7. Then, using all the information they have collected, instruct students to write a brief summary of what they have learned and place this on an index card. This will become Layer 2 in the Pyramid Diagram.
8. The last step is for students to develop a conclusion that relates to the focusing question. To do this, students use the first layer as a title, the second layer as the topic sentence, the third layer to expand on the topic sentence and, finally, the fourth layer to supply details to illustrate the points made.

See Figure 5.14 for an example of a Pyramid Diagram for social studies and Figure 5.22 at the end of the chapter for a blackline master for this strategy.

Example of Pyramid Diagram for Social Studies

Focusing Question:

What was the Holocaust and why did it occur?
World War II was caused by a combination of economic and political factors that were confounded by the creation of two major divisions of allies and fueled by a local conflict between two countries.

What was the Holocaust?		Why did Nazis want to kill large numbers of innocent people?		How did Nazis carry out their policy of genocide?		How did the world respond to the Holocaust?	
Nazi Germany persecuted and annihilated Jews from 1933 to 1945.	Six million Jews were killed. Gypsies, handicapped people, Poles, Soviet prisoners, Communists, Socialists, Freemasons, homosexuals, and Jehovah's Witnesses were also targeted.	Nazis believed Germans were "racially superior," and there was a struggle for survival between them and "inferior races."	Jews, Gypsies, handicapped people, and Slavs were seen as threat to Aryan purity, and they were blamed for the German defeat in WW I. Millions died of starvation, disease, and forced labor or were killed for racial, political reasons.	In the 1930s, they used lethal injection and poison gas.	After Germany invaded the Soviet Union, millions were shot in villages, open fields, etc. Finally extermination centers were created in occupied Poland, where prisoners were gassed and their bodies cremated.	Between 1930 and 1944, the U.S. and England knew about the "Final Solution" but, due to the war effort, anti-Semitism, and fear of refugee influx, they did nothing.	Mounting pressure eventually led the U.S. to begin modified rescue efforts in 1944, but German occupied countries sided with Nazis. Some countries, like Denmark, and individuals helped rescue. Russia, Britain, and France joined forces against Austria, Hungary, and Germany to start war.

Figure 5.14

138

Three Level Guide

The format of the Three Level Guide strategy (Herber, 1978) closely follows the parameters of Raphael, Au, and Highfield's (2006) QAR strategy discussed in Chapter 2. If students have learned and can use the thinking processes embedded in the QAR strategy that help them identify textually explicit and textually implicit questions in their readings, teachers can reinforce these processes by using the Three Level Guide as a strategy to guide students' reading. The first level of Herber's Three Level Guide, the literal level, fosters students' ability to gather important information and corresponds to the QAR's "right there," or textually explicit question; while the second, or inferential level, which asks students to ferret out the author's intended meaning by reading between the lines, making inferences, and drawing conclusions, corresponds to the QAR's "think and search," or textually implicit question; and, finally, Herber's third, or application level, which asks students to apply what they have read to new and different life situations, corresponds to the QAR's "author and you" and "on your own" questions.

Steps for a Three Level Guide

1. First determine the specific ideas and concepts that reflect the author's intended and inferred meaning that you think students should learn from the assigned text.

2. Once these ideas and concepts have been determined, write five to ten statements that reflect them; these statements become Level 2, or the inferential level, of the guide.

3. Next, determine what explicit facts from the reading support the inference statements developed for Level 2, and write these facts as statements. These become the statements for Level 1 of the study guide. Strive to develop at least two literal statements to support each major inference.

4. Then to develop the third level, or applied level, of the guide, construct four to five statements that ask students to make connections between their prior knowledge, or what they already know about a topic, and what they have learned in their reading. In effect, in this level of the guide, students must apply their knowledge to a new situation.

5. Finally, to assure that students focus their thinking as they complete the Three Level Guide, Vacca and Vacca (2008) suggest that distracters, or misleading facts, be incorporated into levels 1 and 2 to discourage students from marking items indiscriminately.

As always, to assure that students fully understand how to successfully utilize the strategy as part of their learning, the teacher should model the strategy as a whole class activity before allowing students to apply it independently. Figure 5.15 shows how the Three Level Guide can be used with language arts or English classes, while Figure 5.16 shows how it can be used with a science topic.

Example of a Three Level Guide for Language Arts/English
Shirley Jackson, "The Lottery"

Part I—Literal Level

Check the statements that are true.

1._____ The lottery takes place each year in the spring.

2._____ All the people collect stones for the lottery.

3._____ Mrs. Delacroix is a good friend of Tessie Hutchinson.

4._____ Tessie Hutchinson is the winner in the lottery.

5._____ Some surrounding villages have stopped holding the lottery.

Part II—Interpretive Level

Check any of the following statements that you think can be inferred from the story.

1._____ Mr. Summers, Mr. Graves, and Mr. Martin hold high social status in the village.

2._____ One of the themes of "The Lottery" is hypocrisy.

3._____ The village follows a democratic process as it conducts the lottery.

4._____ Old Man Warner believes in a strong work ethic.

5._____ Women in the town are considered subordinate to the men.

Part III—Applied Level

Check the items that you think relay the author's message, based on your personal experience.

1._____ People should stand up for what they believe no matter how dangerous it is to do so.

2._____ Old ways die hard.

3._____ We can remain free only so long as we exercise our right to think and act independently of demands society places on us.

4._____ Things look different when the shoe is on the other foot.

5._____ Some things are worth sacrifice.

Figure 5.15

Example of a Three Level
Guide for Science or Health
Bacteria

Part I—Literal Level

Check the statements that are true.

1._____ Bacteria are small organisms that can be found everywhere.

2._____ A virus can be cured.

3._____ If someone is immune to a disease, he or she will never catch that disease.

4._____ A vaccine cures diseases.

5._____ Fungus appears on spoiled food.

Part II—Interpretive Level

Check any of the following statements that you think can be inferred from your reading and lab experiments.

1._____ Fungus grows best in conditions that are warm and moist.

2._____ Protozoans are more similar to plant and animal cells than to bacteria.

3._____ Bacteria are always harmful to people.

4._____ If bacteria build up, it will cause mold and mildew to grow.

5._____ Antibiotics kill good cells as well as the harmful cells they have been designed to kill.

Part III—Applied Level

Check the items you think relay the author's message and are based on what you know or have heard from personal experience. Be ready to explain your answers.

1._____ Antibiotics can be dangerous to people's health.

2._____ All scientific research in the area of medicine is beneficial.

3._____ Due to knowledge of how diseases are transmitted, diseases like the Black Plague that struck the Middle Ages in Europe will never happen again.

4._____ Once a person is vaccinated for a disease, he or she will never catch it.

5._____ The concept "forewarned is forearmed" can be applied to the study of bacteriology.

Figure 5.16

CHAPTER SUMMARY

This chapter's focus is on the Engage the Learner phase of the block schedule lesson plan format, during which students are encouraged to actively interact with and process what they have learned by validating predictions, keeping their purpose for reading in mind, and self-monitoring their understanding. It is during this phase that students utilize instructional frameworks such as study guides, note-taking formats, and graphic organizers to make connections between what they are learning (new knowledge) and what they already know (old knowledge). This chapter provides a myriad of strategies and activities that students can employ to gather comprehension and understanding from the information presented to them during the enticement and enlightenment phases presented in chapters 3 and 4. These specific strategies and activities are presented in two categories: strategies for monitoring learning, such as SMART and INSERT; and strategies for guiding learning, such as Guided Note Taking, Reader's Questions, the 5W Model, Extended Anticipation Guide, About/Point, Magnet Summary, Sketch to Stretch, Jot Charts, Pyramid Diagram, and Three Level Guide.

BLACKLINE MASTERS

Blackline masters for implementing the strategies in this chapter may be found on pages 142 through 148.

Reader's Questions

Directions: As you read about the topic assigned, complete the graphic organizer by providing information to answer the following questions:

1. Who or what is the topic? If it is a person, name the person and list key people in his or her life. If it is a topic, name significant people associated with the topic.

2. When and where did the topic take place? Or, when and where did the person live, travel, and become a success?

3. What were the person's beliefs? Or, what were the topic's main elements?

4. How did the person relate to others? Solve problems? Achieve recognition? Or, how did the topic become recognized and successful?

5. Why was the person or topic important?

Who or What:

When and Where: (Time and Place)	What: (Beliefs or Elements)	What: (Problems)	How: (Solutions, Recognition)	Why: (Was the Topic, Person Important)

Figure 5.17

Source: From *Reading and Writing Across Content Areas* (2nd ed., p. 178), by R. L. Sejnost and S. Thiese, 2007, Thousand Oaks, CA: Corwin. Copyright © 2007 by Corwin. Reprinted with permission.

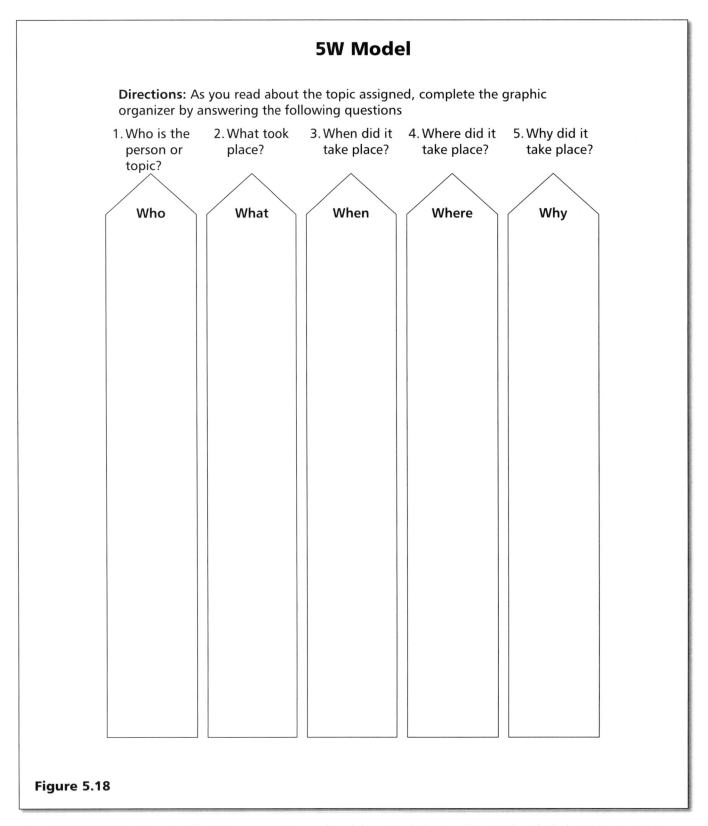

5W Model

Directions: As you read about the topic assigned, complete the graphic organizer by answering the following questions

1. Who is the person or topic?
2. What took place?
3. When did it take place?
4. Where did it take place?
5. Why did it take place?

Who   What   When   Where   Why

Figure 5.18

About/Point

Directions: Read the assigned passage and write a sentence that tells what the passage was about, its MAIN IDEA. Next, list up to seven points that support or tell more about the main idea.

This reading is about:

And the points that support it are as follows:

1.

2.

3.

4.

5.

6.

7.

Figure 5.19

Source: From Reading and Writing Across Content Areas (2nd ed., p. 133), by R. L. Sejnost and S. Thiese, 2007, Thousand Oaks, CA: Corwin. Copyright © 2007 by Corwin. Reprinted with permission.

Magnet Summary

KEYWORDS

———————   ———————   ———————   ———————

MAGNET WORD

KEYWORDS

———————   ———————   ———————   ———————

SUMMARY

Figure 5.20

Source: From *Reading and Writing Across Content Areas* (2nd ed., p. 177), by R. L. Sejnost and S. Thiese, 2007, Thousand Oaks, CA: Corwin. Copyright © 2007 by Corwin. Reprinted with permission.

Sketch to Stretch

Directions:

1. Listen as your teacher reads a section of text aloud to you. As you listen, try to make a picture in your mind of what the words are saying and sketch what comes to your mind in the **SKETCH** column in the graphic organizer below.

2. After you have completed your sketch, your teacher will give you a copy of the text. Reread it and add details or revisions to your drawing.

3. Next, pair with a classmate to share and interpret your drawings for one another.

4. Finally, together decide what important facts you can write to summarize the information shown in your picture. Write this in the **SUMMARY OF IMPORTANT POINTS** column of the graphic organizer.

Sketch	Summary of Important Points
Sketch	Summary of Important Points
Sketch	Summary of Important Points
Sketch	Summary of Important Points

Figure 5.21

Pyramid Diagram

Focusing Question: _____

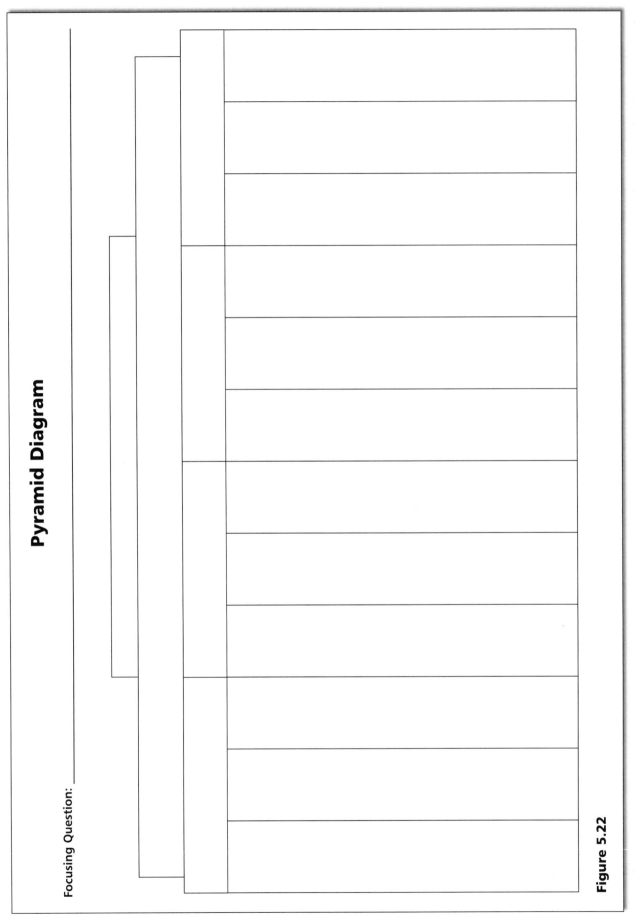

Figure 5.22

CHAPTER 6

Extend the Learner

No matter how good teaching may be, each student must take the responsibility for his own education.

—John Carolus, SJ

THE FOURTH PHASE: EXTENSION

In the previous chapter, the third phase of the lesson plan format, Engage the Learner, was discussed. This chapter will focus on the fourth phase of an effective lesson plan for learning in the block, Extend the Learner. This phase lasts approximately 20 to 25 minutes and is grounded in the facets of a brain-compatible classroom as outlined by Williams and Dunn (2008) and discussed in Chapter 2, specifically facets 1, 4, 5, 6, 7, 8, and 9. During this phase, students need to clarify and reinforce what they have learned by organizing, synthesizing, analyzing, and evaluating what they have read so they can easily understand and retrieve important information and then reflect, apply, and act on it. In other words, this phase of the lesson planning format encourages students to extend their learning through reflection and action. As Richardson and Morgan (2003) note, it is this reflection on learning that helps students clarify their thinking and focus their understanding so they can better retain and act upon what they have learned because the more one reflects on what has been read and learned, the longer it will be remembered and the more likely it is that the information will be used. Furthermore, they posit that additional by-products of this reflection phase are that students become critical thinkers and autonomous or independent learners.

As teachers, we can readily see that the three by-products of the Extend the Learner phase—(1) retention of learning, (2) critical thinking, and (3) deliberate action—lead students along the path to becoming autonomous learners, a status that we all desire for our students. In addition, Cioffi (1992) stresses that, although teachers can isolate important facts for their students as they teach them, the students must, on their own, determine whether those facts are worthwhile and how to act upon them. In effect, to do this they must become critical thinkers, effective reflectors, and active doers. Roe, Stoodt-Hill, and Burns (2007) provide a clear profile of exactly what a critical thinker is. In effect, critical thinkers are open-minded and avoid making judgments until all facts have been verified. They constantly question the content they are studying and face each learning/thinking task with a problem-solving attitude. They evaluate the material they read for its validity and its content, such as the use of logic, propaganda, and language, as well as for the author's qualifications and purpose for writing.

In my experience, the most efficient way to assure that students become critical thinkers and independent learners and active doers is to allow them, after moving through the enticement, enlightenment, and engagement phases discussed in previous chapters of this text, to engage in this final extension phase, where the student remembers what has been read and learned, thinks critically about it, and, in reflection, evaluates its worth and, finally, acts upon it. If students efficiently engage in this final phase, they will come naturally to the stage of independent or autonomous learners. They will become what we want them to become: lifelong learners.

Thus, one can easily see the power of the Extend the Learner phase in the process of empowering students to become the lifelong learners we want them to be. However, many times teachers ask students to engage in this phase of their learning by merely taking quizzes or tests. While this practice may check whether students have read and learned and then remembered what they have read and learned, it fails to empower them to be critical thinkers and independent learners. In fact, Wood (1996) suggests that such assessments may not be effective in the learning climates of today, which, in fact, strive to foster higher-level thinking and integrated curricula. Thus, for students to be successful critical thinkers and independent learners, they must be able to evaluate what they have read, questioning it with an open mind. They need to consider its validity, its value, its purpose, and its logic. These skills are not easily fostered through only taking quizzes and tests. Instead, to foster critical thinking and independent learning, students must be allowed to show what they have learned in more authentic ways. Linn, Baker, and Dunbar (1991) note that authentic assessments enhance student learning and lead to higher student achievement. Thus, this chapter will provide specific after-learning strategies such as discussions, presentations, writing activities, research activities, and performances that are connected to or can be transferred to real-life applications, which are authentic in nature.

STRATEGIES AND ACTIVITIES TO USE TO EXTEND THE LEARNER

Learning Journals and Logs

Learning journals and logs provide a variety of dimensions for students to apply what they have learned. According to Zemelman and Daniels (1988), journal and log writing fosters a myriad of skills and abilities, such as note taking and documentation skills as well as vocabulary and writing skills. But, Buehl (2001) reminds us that students often have difficulty processing what they have learned into their own words, and Commander and Smith (1996) suggest that, through the use of journals and logs, students can become more metacognitively aware and thus more adroit at monitoring their understanding. Overall, according to Irvin, Buehl, and Radcliffe (2007), the use of journals and logs not only allows students to record the "what" of learning but also to reflect on, and thus process, the "how" and the "why" of what they are learning. As Sejnost and Thiese (2007) note, using learning journals and logs in the classroom is an effective way to invite students to respond, reflect, question, and react to the material in their text and to connect to their thoughts and feelings. In addition, students can record their ideas in several ways, including listing (list as many insects as possible), drawing (draw the bunkhouse), and questioning (what is statistical analysis?) as well as recording reactions (what are some reasons for supporting/ opposing the war?) and point-of-view responses (assume the persona of . . .). Finally, Vacca and Vacca (2008) remind us that for learning journals and logs to be truly effective after-learning strategies, they must be used regularly. In addition, Buehl (2001) stresses that since learning journals and learning logs require reflective writing, a process students may not be familiar or comfortable with, it is crucial that teachers model the process for them. As we assign journals and logs, Burke (2005) reminds us that log entries should be short, impersonal, objective entries that might concisely report facts such as "mathematical problem-solving entries, lists of outside readings, homework assignments, or anything that lends itself to keeping records" (p. 120), while journals are "usually more descriptive, longer, open ended and more free-flowing . . ." (p. 120) and can be used to respond and reflect on personal experiences and feelings about what is being learned.

Double-Entry Journal

In the Double-Entry Journal strategy (Vaughan, 1990), students utilize their note-taking and documentation skills to record information from a text, lecture, video, or something similar and then use metacognitive awareness to reflect on it, thereby fostering their critical thinking skills and encouraging them to be independent learners as they think about the content and their reactions to it in order to respond to and reflect on its possible meanings.

Steps for the Double-Entry Journal

1. Students read pages or sections of chapters or listen to a lecture or view a video or CD.

2. They then record key ideas, passages, or quotes and the page number from the text on the left-hand side of the page.

3. Finally, after they have completed the left-hand side of their journal, they use the right-hand side of the page to reflect on what they have written, recording their own feelings, ideas, thoughts, or questions about the passage. See Figure 6.1 for an example of a Double-Entry Journal for social studies and Figure 6.21 at the end of the chapter for a blackline master of the strategy.

Example of Double-Entry Journal for Social Studies

Directions: As you read, note ideas, passages, or quotes that seem to stand out to you. They may surprise you, provide you with information you did not know before, or just make you think. Write them in Column 1 of the graphic organizer below. Write the page(s) where these ideas or quotes were found in Column 2. Then, in Column 3, record your response to what you read.

Key Ideas, Passages, or Quotes	Page Number	Feelings, Questions, and Concerns
Over 100,000 children were hidden and thus protected from the Nazis.	19	How long did they have to hide? It must have been very frightening for these children.
Both Jewish and Gypsy children suffered during the Holocaust.	46	Wow! I didn't realize that other groups besides the Jewish people were discriminated against. I wonder what other groups suffered and why we usually only hear about or remember the Jews.

Figure 6.1

CONVERSATIONS

An effective way to help students cement their learning into long-term memory is to ask them to think about what they have learned, analyzing, synthesizing, reflecting, and weaving it all into a parcel of knowledge they can share with others in a discussion format. Grand Conversations, Instructional Conversations, Poster Sessions, and Save the Last Word for Me are all strategies that give students practice in doing this.

Grand Conversations

Grand Conversations (Eeds & Wells, 1989, and Peterson & Eeds, 1990, as described in Tompkins, 2004) encourage students to engage in a deep conversation about a narrative they have read. During a Grand Conversation, students are free to explore how they have interpreted the text and share what reflections they have had about it both during and after reading. Grand Conversations take place with students seated in a circle to facilitate easily seeing one another, and while the teacher serves as the facilitator of the conversation, the focus is on a dialogue between students.

Steps for a Grand Conversation

1. After reading a book, students record their thoughts and feelings in a journal, log, Quickwrite, or Quickdraw. (Note: These last two strategies will be discussed in specific later in this chapter.)
2. Then students gather, either as an entire class or in prearranged small groups, to discuss the book according to the following topics:
   a. events in the plot
   b. author's language, style, craft
   c. outstanding or favorite quotes
   d. illustrations
3. During the conversation, students are encouraged to refer to their journals, logs, Quickwrites, or Quickdraws as they discuss the book, and they are also encouraged to build upon the thoughts, ideas, and comments of others as they proceed through the conversation.
4. After students have had ample opportunity to discuss their thoughts and reflections, the teacher, as facilitator, asks open-ended questions to bring the students' attention to any important aspect of the book that has not yet been discussed.
5. Finally, students should be encouraged to reflect on the Grand Conversation process by adding to their reading journals or logs.

Instructional Conversations

The Instructional Conversations strategy (Goldenberg, 1992–1993, as described in Tompkins, 2004) is similar to the Grand Conversation strategy discussed above, except it is utilized when students read expository text rather than narrative text. In Instructional Conversations, students focus on the main ideas they have learned about a topic, and, as in Grand Conversations, students are encouraged to actively participate while the teacher, as facilitator, clarifies misinformation, asks high-level focusing questions, and provides instructional information to help students grasp the topic being studied, all the while encouraging students to go back into the text to provide specific references to support their responses.

Steps for an Instructional Conversation

1. To prepare for an Instructional Conversation, the teacher identifies and informs the students of the focus of the topic that will be discussed.

2. After studying the topic, students record their thoughts and feelings about the designated focus in a journal, log, Quickwrite, or Quickdraw. (Note: These last two strategies will be discussed in specific later in this chapter.)

3. Then students gather, either as an entire class or in prearranged small groups, to discuss the topic using the focus determined by the teacher.

4. As students present their thoughts, questions, and opinions, the teacher records their responses so they can be shared at a later time.

5. Once students have completed a discussion of the focused topic, the teacher encourages students to consider other aspects of the topic as well to make personal connections to the topic.

6. Finally, students should be encouraged to reflect on the Instructional Conversation process by adding to their reading journals or logs.

Poster Session

The Poster Session strategy (Silver, Strong, & Perini, 2001) is a creative way of helping students think, reflect, present, and exchange ideas about a topic that has been studied. For this strategy, students can either work individually or in small groups to present the main concepts or big ideas as well as their reflections on them via a poster designed to include both pictures and words as a short narrative to accompany their visual display. Stress to students, however, that their poster must be completely self-explanatory. Once the posters are completed, they are hung around the classroom, and students circulate to view the thoughts and reflections of their classmates. As a final step, students convene as a whole class to discuss what they have learned.

Steps for Poster Session

1. After studying a topic, students choose a concept or idea related to it that can be presented in a visual format.

2. Silver, Strong, and Perini (2001) suggest that students understand that the poster must meet the following criteria: It must be (a) self-explanatory, (b) clear, (c) comprehensive, (d) colorful, and (e) creative.

3. When the visuals are completed, they are posted around the classroom, and students circulate, view, and discuss the creations.

4. Finally, as a whole class, students review what they have learned and add their new learning and reflections to their reading logs or journals.

Save the Last Word for Me

Another strategy that is designed to help students become both critical and reflective in their thinking and learning is Save the Last Word for Me (Burke & Harste as discussed in Buehl, 2001). Buehl suggests that this strategy is best utilized when the text assignment might offer students differing interpretations or draw out differing opinions. Furthermore, Buehl notes that if Save the Last Word for Me is done in a small group setting rather then in a whole class setting, students who may be reluctant to share their differing or opposing ideas and opinions are usually more apt to do so. Finally, he suggests that since this strategy asks students to prepare their thoughts and reflections ahead of time by writing them down on index cards, even the most reluctant student is given some rehearsal time to prepare before being asked to present.

Below is an example of Save the Last Word for Me for narrative writing:

The statement: "The policeman on the beat moved up the avenue impressively. The impressiveness was habitual and not for show, for spectators were few."

The last word: The description of the policeman really made me understand why he could fool Bob so easily. He was so used to acting like a policeman that he simply acted out of habit, so Bob never suspected that the policeman was his good friend. What a neat surprise ending that made!

And here is an example for expository writing:

The statement: "Thousands and thousands of square miles of jungle are destroyed each year when farmers burn down trees to increase the amount of land to farm."

The last word: While the burning of jungles helps the farmer's economic situation, what effect does it have on the world? When jungles are destroyed, exotic animals and plants are destroyed as well. Some of them may even fall into extinction.

Steps for Save the Last Word for Me

1. After reading either an expository or narrative assignment, have students reread to locate at least five statements that appeal to them

because they (a) are interesting; (b) are contradictory to or supportive of the students' thoughts, beliefs, or established knowledge; (c) surprised or intrigued the students; or (d) in some way revealed new knowledge to the students.

2. Students should then record each of these statements and its location in the text on the front side of index card.

3. On the reverse side of the index card, students should write down their thoughts and reflections about the statement as well as comment on why they chose the statement.

4. Once the index cards have been completed, students may move into small groups to share. Sharing follows this format:

   a. The first student reads a statement and provides its location in the text, so all members of the group may read it.

   b. After reading the chosen statement, each student in the small group comments on it, giving his or her thoughts and ideas.

   c. After listening to all the group members' thoughts and reflections, the originating student shares his or her thoughts and reflections, thereby "saving the last word for me." As Buehl states, "The attitude during this phase is: Here is a statement that interested me. You tell me what you think, and then I will tell you what I think" (p. 122).

   d. This process of sharing thoughts and reflections is repeated until all of the statements have been presented.

EXTENDED FORMAT RESPONSES

As noted earlier, multiple-choice, true-false, and short-answer quizzes and tests do not always effectively measure what students have learned, because they require students to use only factual information and rote memory. While learning journals and logs are one way to foster students' critical and reflective thinking abilities, three other strategies, Quickwrites, Quickdraws, and the One Minute Paper provide the same opportunity in an extended format. Each of these strategies will be discussed in detail below.

Quickwrites

Quickwrites (Tompkins, 2002) ask students, after reading, to reflect on what they have learned about a topic as well as to clarify what connections among ideas they can make. This strategy, first developed by Elbow (1973), concentrates on what students say rather than how it is said. In other words, the focus should be on the content students present rather than on the mechanics they use as they write.

Quickdraws

Quickdraws (Tompkins, 2004) are similar in nature, but in this strategy students draw rather than write about what they have learned.

Steps for Quickwrites and Quickdraws

1. Students read pages or sections of chapters, or listen to a lecture, or view a video or CD.

2. They then write or draw the key or interesting ideas in the passages, making connections between the topic and their own lives and reflecting on the connections.

3. Once students have finished their Quickwrites or Quickdraws, they may share with their small groups or the entire class.

4. If they share, they may then revise or add to what they have written or drawn by adding information they have learned through their sharing experience.

See Figure 6.2 for an example of a Quickwrite and a Quickdraw.

Example of Quickwrite and Quickdraw for Science

Quickwrite for the Concept of Solids

Solids = are rigid with definite shapes because the particles that make them up are strongly attracted to one another and packed closely together. The volume of solids is constant even under very high pressure and changes only a little bit when the temperature changes.

Quickdraw for the Concept of Solids

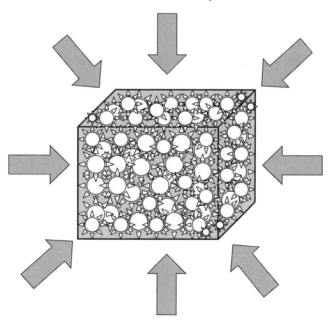

Figure 6.2

One Minute Papers

The One Minute Paper (Weaver and Cotrell, 1985; Wilson, 1986) actually takes several minutes and often focuses on questions such as, "What did you learn about _____ today?" and "What questions do you still have?" As in the Quickwrites and Quickdraws, students are encouraged to synthesize what they have learned and then reflect on it. Utilizing the One Minute Paper fosters the students' ability to review what they have learned, focusing on the key concepts and encapsulating it in their own words, which heightens their metacognitive awareness. Finally, it also fosters their writing abilities. As a side note, while students may complete the One Minute Paper individually, Cross and Angelo (1988) suggest students work in pairs and exchange their papers in order to compare and discuss their responses.

CREATIVE AFTER-LEARNING STRATEGIES

The strategies previously discussed are, in fact, rather controlled methods to allow students to exhibit what they have learned. However, there are also a variety of more creative strategies that will accomplish the same thing. These more creative after-learning strategies include the following: Alphabet Catch, A to Z–Connect to Me, ABC Book, the Biography Poem, the Biography Cinquain, the Fact Acrostic, and RAFT.

The ABC Summary

The alphabet, a format easily remembered by students, also serves as an excellent trigger for remembering important ideas, facts, and information about a topic that has been studied. There are several alphabet-based strategies that can be used to help students process the information they have learned. In effect, students connect words or phrases related to a topic they have been studying to the letters of the alphabet. This can be done in a variety of ways:

1. **Alphabet Catch:** In this strategy, students choose a letter of the alphabet at random. After selecting a letter, students make a connection between the topic studied and the letter selected and then develop a short response, a sentence, or a paragraph summarizing and explaining the connection that was made. The responses are then shared with the entire class.

2. **A to Z–Connect to Me:** This strategy is similar to the Alphabet Catch strategy discussed above. However, rather than making a connection to a single letter of the alphabet, this strategy asks students to work individually or in groups to connect all the letters of the alphabet to

the topic studied and then create a sentence or a paragraph for each that explains the connection.

3. **ABC Alphabet Book:** Yet another strategy that takes the alphabet strategy a step further is the creation of an alphabet book based on the topic studied. The creation of such a book is not only a creative and engaging activity for students, but once it is completed, it can be shared with younger students in a peer tutoring adventure. An outline of how students can create such a book is provided in Figure 6.3, while a checklist for assessing an ABC book can be found in Figure 6.22 at the end of this chapter.

Example of ABC Book Assignment

Alphabet Book Project

After studying our current unit, you will summarize your knowledge by creating an alphabet book using the following guidelines:

Topics—You will choose a topic related to our current unit of study. For each letter of the alphabet, you will develop one to two sentences that explain something about the entry. For example, in studying Lincoln, if the alphabet letter is H, you might write "Herndon, Lincoln's law partner when they were lawyers in Springfield, Illinois." Here is an example of an Alphabet Book for World War I:

A. Austria
B. Britain
C. Coalitions
D. Division of Europe
E. Economic causes
F. France
G. Germany
H. Hungary
I. Italy

J. Japan
K. Krupp
L. Leaders
M. Mexican alliance
N. National power
O. Ottoman Empire
P. Portugal
Q. Quantity killed
R. Russia

S. Sarajevo
T. Tension caused by?
U. U.S.A.
V. Victory
W. Western front
X. Axis of Powers
Y. Years fought
Z. Zero hour

Guidelines: The project must include

1. cover with title, author, and an illustration.
2. dedication.

(Continued)

(Continued)

3. a publisher and copyright date.

4. text—one page per letter.

5. illustrations—You may illustrate using any media you wish: drawings, computer graphics, photographs you have taken yourself, magazine pictures. Strive to use as many different kinds of illustrative materials as you can.

6. author page—Include a brief biography that could provide the following information:
   a. Where you were born—city, state, country
   b. Your family—sisters, brothers, pets, hobbies you have
   c. Your year in school
   d. Your plans for the future; Work—if/where you work now
   e. A picture of yourself

Tips for Writing:

1. Be sure you do a rough draft and have it approved before doing illustrations.

2. Make sure your hands are clean when you work on your books. Avoid using crayons; they smear.

3. Keep your "book in progress" in the folder assigned to you.

4. If you are hand-writing your book, use a liner to keep the printing straight.

5. Print, write, or draw lightly in case you wish to erase something.

6. Be creative with your method of illustrating; your pictures don't have to be perfect.

Tips for Oral Reading: When your book is completed, you will read it to the class. To do a good job, you should

1. practice reading your book aloud several times; read to your siblings or a friend, in front of a mirror, and so forth.

2. practice reading slowly, loudly, and clearly.

3. make sure you know all the words in your story and can explain anything that might be unfamiliar.

4. read with expression.

5. make eye contact as you read.

6. show your illustrations.

Figure 6.3

Biography Poem

The Biography Poem (Gere, 1985) is yet another effective after-reading strategy that requires students to focus on important concepts of a topic and then follow a specific formula to compose a biographic poem featuring those concepts. As with previously described critical thinking and reflective thinking strategies, the Biography Poem requires students to synthesize what they have learned about a subject into a relatively short poetic format (Vacca & Vacca, 2002). In effect, this strategy fosters students' ability to consolidate, integrate, and synthesize new information while encouraging them to think actively and reflect rather than merely writing answers to questions. See Figure 6.4 for an example of a Biography Poem for science and Figure 6.5 for a Biography Poem for Spanish. Finally, see Figure 6.23 at the end of the chapter for a blackline master for the Biography Poem.

Steps for a Biography Poem

1. Have students use the Biography Poem formula detailed in the blackline master, Figure 6.23, to create a poem that applies to any content area topic.
2. Students can illustrate the poem with pictures or photographs.

Example of Biography Poem for Science

Pollution

Impairs vision, irritates lungs, damages nervous system, contributes to acid rain

Relative of auto exhaust

Lover of carbon monoxide, nitrogen dioxide, sulfur dioxide

Who feels harsh, damaging, irritating

Who needs auto exhaust, factories, oil refineries

Who fears government regulation, inspections, lawsuits

Who gives illness, respiratory problems, lung damage

Who would like to see more factories, paper mills, and power plants

Resident of United States

Last name Death

Figure 6.4

Example of Biography Poem for Spanish

Frida

Strong, high-spirited, bold, committed

Wife of Diego Rivera

Lover of: surrealism, revolution, monkeys

Who feels: pain constantly, sad she has no children, sympathetic toward communism

Who needs to: paint realistically, be rebellious, share her Mexican heritage

Who fears: her painting will not be appreciated, Americans dislike her, she will never be well

Who gives: the world great art, support to Leon Trotsky, love to Diego Rivera

Who would like to see: successful revolutions, herself in portraits, her art respected

Resident of Coyoacán

Kahlo

Figure 6.5

Biography Cinquain

An alternative to the Biography Poem is the Biography Cinquain (Sejnost & Thiese, 2007), which can be used when class time is short, as an introductory activity before students write the lengthier Biography Poem, or with students who may need practice with a less demanding assignment than the Biography Poem. To develop a Biography Cinquain, students need only to follow the "recipe" detailed in the blackline master shown in Figure 6.24 at the end of the chapter. Figure 6.6 provides an example of a Biography Cinquain for business.

Example of Biography Cinquain for Business

Internet

Accessible, resourceful

Electronic, navigable, infinite

A vast collection of resources

Internet

Figure 6.6

Fact Acrostic

The acrostic is a frequently used word game in which letters are written down the margin of a paper, one letter per line, and then descriptions beginning with the appropriate letter are written to match. The Fact Acrostic is a variation of this popular form that asks students to use topics found in the content area for the terms and to create an acrostic by describing facts and ideas that are related to the topic (Johnston, 1985). The true value of this strategy lies in the fact that since students may need to reread the text to complete the acrostic, they will enhance their own knowledge about the topic while using their creative abilities to transfer the information into a poetic form.

Steps for a Fact Acrostic

1. Instruct students to write the letters of the content area topic down the left margin of a page.
2. Have students write a fact about the topic in each line of the poem.

Figure 6.7 provides a Fact Acrostic for English or language arts while Figure 6.8 provides an example for social studies.

Example of Fact Acrostic for English/Language Arts

SCOUT

Searches for the truth

Confused by events that surround her

Outgoing

Unwilling to overlook events

Totally committed

Figure 6.7

Example of Fact Acrostic for Social Studies

PRESIDENT

*P*eople's choice

*R*ules with House and Senate

*E*nacts policy

*S*tate of the Union address

*I*naugurated in January

*D*irects cabinet

*E*levates judges to Supreme Court

*N*o vote is a veto

*T*erm of office is four years

Figure 6.8

RAFT

Yet another strategy that asks students to think critically and reflect while they synthesize what they have learned is RAFT (Santa, 1988), which is an acronym for Role, Audience, Format, and Topic.

R = Role of the writer (Who are you as the writer? What role do you play?)

A = Audience for the writer (To whom are you writing? Who will read your writing?)

F = Format of the writing (What form will your writing take?)

T = Topic of the writing (What will you be writing about?)

The RAFT strategy is effective, for it fosters both critical thinking and reflection as it not only requires students to consider a topic from a perspective different from their own but also asks them to write for a specific audience and in a specific format as well. In addition, as Buehl (2001) notes, "RAFT is a method that works to infuse imagination, creativity, and motivation into a writing assignment" (p. 114). As always, however, for best results, the teacher should model this strategy before students use it independently.

Steps for RAFT

1. First, students must analyze the important ideas, concepts, or information from the reading assignment. This will determine the topic of the assignment.

2. Next, with students, brainstorm possible roles class members could assume in their writing. This will determine the role for the assignment.

3. Then, ask students to determine the audience for this writing.

4. Finally, the format of the writing must be determined.

As a suggestion, when first assigning the RAFT strategy, it might be more efficient to assign all students to the same role for their writing. In subsequent lessons, students can be encouraged to brainstorm their own roles, audiences, and formats. See Figure 6.9 for an example of the RAFT strategy for social studies and Figure 6.10 for a list of possible RAFT assignments.

Example for RAFT for Social Studies

Role = a news journalist

Audience = newspaper readers

Format = a news story

Topic = assassination of John F. Kennedy

On Friday, November 22, 1963, President John F. Kennedy was assassinated in Dallas, Texas. President Kennedy, riding in an open-air convertible with his wife, Jackie, and Texas governor John Connally and his wife, was shot by Lee Harvey Oswald, who shot him from the window of the Texas Book Depository.

According to witnesses, the shots rang out just as Kennedy's limousine turned from Houston Avenue onto Elm Street. President Kennedy suffered massive wounds to his head and was rushed to Parkland Hospital, where he was officially pronounced dead at 1:00 p.m. Governor Connally suffered wounds to his back, chest, wrist, and left thigh but survived.

Lee Harvey Oswald was seen leaving the Despository lunchroom only minutes after the shooting, and, at 11:36 p.m., was arrested and charged with JFK's murder. Jack Ruby, in a self-proclaimed attempt to spare Jacqueline Kennedy, the President's wife, the ordeal of a trial, shot Oswald to death as millions of television viewers watched.

Figure 6.9

Topics for RAFT

Role	Audience	Format	Topic
for Mathematics			
triangle	circle	resume	presenting attributes, experiences, abilities
parentheses	algebraic equation	love letter	what parentheses can do for equations
journalist	public	news release	steps in solving a linear equation
coach	basketball player	play book	geometric attributes of a basketball court
for Science			
fiction author	children	a narrative	why you have brown eyes rather blue ones
archeologist	chemical company	instructional pamphlet	use of diffusion/osmosis in mummification
advertiser	magazine publisher	infomercial	how to prevent MRSA
cheeseburger	fat cell	travel guide	journey through the digestive system and blood to the heart
for Social Studies			
constituent	US senator	letter	gun control
presidential candidate	the American people	speech	position on immigration policy
cartoon journalist	newspaper readers	political cartoon	current political issue
researcher	lawyers	survey and analysis of results	pros and cons of the death penalty
for English/Language Arts			
chef	English teachers	recipe	making Hamlet a successful production
Ben Franklin	people of the colonies	memoirs	his experiments and adventures
Thoreau	Brook Farm residents	essay	elements of transcendentalism
Brutus	people of Rome	letter	why Julius Caesar had to die
for other subjects			
publicist	sports fans	baseball card	baseball player's statistics
Jenny Craig	obese person	brochure	healthy eating
famous industrialist	his employees	dialogue	how a cell and a factory are similar
artist	museum patrons	chart	comparison of still life painting to landscape painting

Figure 6.10

EMPLOYING DIFFERENT PERSPECTIVES

As discussed earlier, in the Extend the Learner stage of the lesson format, students should synthesize, analyze, and evaluate what they have read, thus clarifying their thinking. In addition, they need to employ both their critical thinking and reflective skills, abilities they will need to become autonomous, lifelong learners. A particularly effective skill that independent learners need to foster is the ability to view a topic or issue from a variety of perspectives, choose a position regarding it, and then be ready to explain and defend that position. The Corners, Human Graph, Cubing, Perspective Cubing, and Discussion Web strategies foster students' ability to do this.

Corners

Corners (Kagan, Robertson, & Kagan, 1995) is a strategy that encourages students to think about a series of issues relating to the content they are studying. In addition, it is a vehicle which fosters students' abilities to clarify their own thoughts and values as well as to provide them with an avenue to thinking through making decisions before acting upon them, a skill that is invaluable to mature behavior because it requires students to make choices, articulate their reasons for those choices, share their choices, and, finally, listen carefully as their peers share their choices and then possibly adapt and change their original positions. This strategy can also help teachers assess their students' understanding of the content being studied.

Steps for Corners

1. Choose an issue on which students can take a variety of positions.

2. Next, designate a specific corner of the classroom for each position on the issue. Label them strongly agree, agree, disagree, and strongly disagree.

3. Next, instruct students to consider the various positions and, without discussing it with their classmates, choose a position and record it on paper with their reasons for making that choice.

4. Finally, ask students to move to the corner that designates their choice and, in pairs, discuss their position and the thinking that led them to their choice.

5. Once students have completed the first round of discussion, they leave their original group of choice to join another group of choice

and, in pairs, once again share their decisions and thoughts with pairs from that group.

6. As students interact with others, encourage them to adapt or change their positions based on what they have learned in their discussions with others.

7. As a final step, instruct the groups to reassemble into their original group of choice and choose a spokesperson who will summarize the reasons for choosing each position.

An interesting aspect of Corners is that is can really be applied to any aspect of any content studied. Below are some possible topics for the Corners strategy:

- science: Bacteria is a dominant species; it will outlast man.
- social studies: The death penalty should be abolished.
- family and consumer science: Couples should attend parenting classes before they are allowed to have a child.
- English/language arts: Hester Prynne should never have been made to wear a scarlet letter.
- health: Every student should be given a mandatory drug test.
- driver's education: The driving age should be raised to 21 years of age.
- business: The Macintosh platform is better than the PC platform.

The Human Graph

The Human Graph strategy, as presented in Fogarty (2001), is similar to Corners, except in this strategy, students line up along an invisible line according to where they stand on a particular issue. As with Corners, in this strategy, students employ both critical thinking and reflection to evaluate their thoughts concerning a topic or issue, think through possible decisions, make a choice, and stand up for their choice ready to explain and defend it.

Steps for the Human Graph

1. Choose an issue on which students can exhibit a variety of levels of knowledge.

2. Next, instruct the students to arrange themselves along an invisible line that represents a continuum of knowledge of 1 to 10

with 1 representing no knowledge and 10 representing expert knowledge.

3. Students then pair themselves together choosing a partner from the opposite end of the continuum and discuss what they know about the topic.

Cubing

The Cubing strategy, first developed by Cowen and Cowen in 1980, is yet another strategy that encourages students to utilize their critical and reflective thinking skills to examine a topic from various aspects. In this activity, students utilize a six-sided cube with one of the following six phrases written on each side: "describe it," "compare it," "associate it," "analyze it," "apply it," and "argue for or against it." They then reflect on what they have learned and respond orally or in writing from one or more of these perspectives.

Steps for Cubing

1. Introduce the topic and the six perspectives from which it might be considered. (Note: Be sure to carefully clarify for students the difference between comparing/contrasting the topic to something and associating it with something.)

2. Next, allow students five minutes to consider each side of the cube.

3. Finally, ask students to talk or write about the topic from any one of the six possible aspects. (Note: You may assign students to a perspective based on their level of academic achievement, or you may ask students to merely toss the cube and respond to whichever perspective lands on top in their toss.)

See Figure 6.25 at the end of the chapter for a blackline master of how to create a cube and Figure 6.11 for an example of Cubing for social studies.

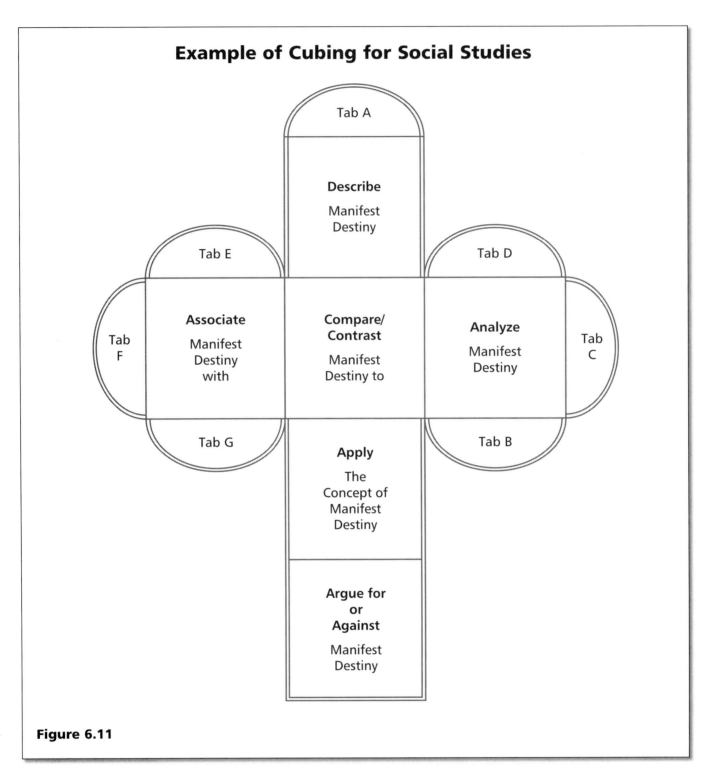

Example of Cubing for Social Studies

Figure 6.11

Source: Cube form adapted from R. G. Meyer and the Southern Regional Educational Technology and Training Center, Mays Landing, New Jersey.

Perspective Cubing

Perspective Cubing (Whitehead, 1994) is a learning strategy that utilizes a twist on the original cubing strategy, because it asks students to apply critical and reflective thinking strategies to a graphic such as a map, chart, graph, or picture, and consider it from the following perspectives, each written on one facet of a cube: space, time, location, culture, talk, and size.

Steps for Perspective Cubing

1. Ask students to study a graphic such as a map, chart, graph, or picture from the text studied and reflect on it from one of the following perspectives:
   a. What might it look like from space?
   b. How would it appear in a different time frame?
   c. What would it look like if it were in a different location?
   d. How would it be different if it were related to a different culture?
   e. What would it say if it could talk?
   f. What would be different if it differed in size? If it were larger? If it were smaller?

2. As in the Cubing strategy, give students five minutes to consider each side of the cube before they talk or write about the topic from any one of the six possible aspects. (Note: You may assign students to a perspective based on their level of academic achievement, or you may ask students to merely toss the cube and respond to whichever perspective lands on top in their toss.)

See Figure 6.12 for an example of Perspective Cubing for science and Figure 6.26 at the end of the chapter for a blackline master for a cube diagram.

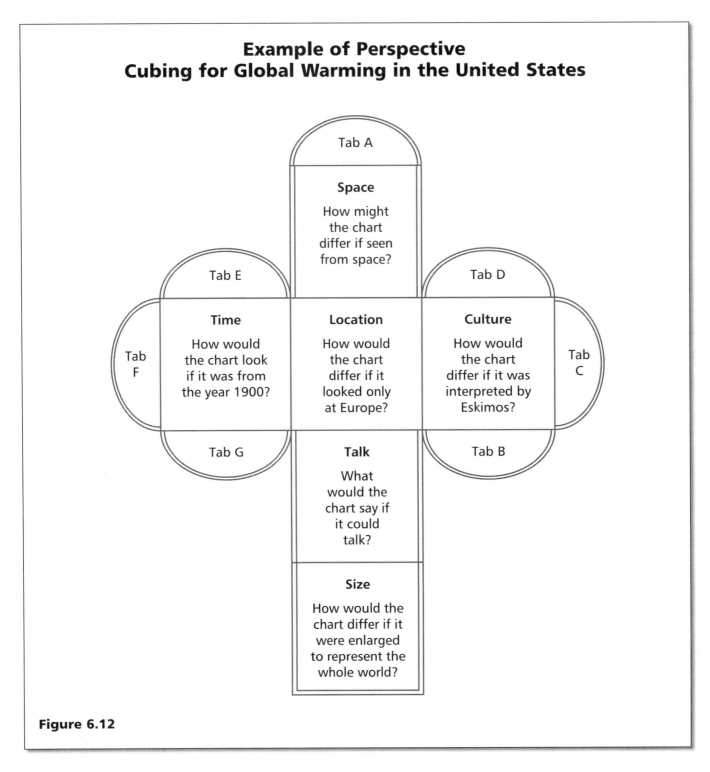

Example of Perspective
Cubing for Global Warming in the United States

Tab A

Space

How might the chart differ if seen from space?

Tab E

Tab D

Time

How would the chart look if it was from the year 1900?

Location

How would the chart differ if it looked only at Europe?

Culture

How would the chart differ if it was interpreted by Eskimos?

Tab F

Tab C

Tab G

Talk

What would the chart say if it could talk?

Tab B

Size

How would the chart differ if it were enlarged to represent the whole world?

Figure 6.12

Source: Cube form adapted from R. G. Meyer and the Southern Regional Educational Technology and Training Center, Mays Landing, New Jersey.

Discussion Web

The Discussion Web (Alvermann, 1991) is a strategy that encourages students to examine an issue from alternative viewpoints, thereby fostering reflection and critical thinking while promoting active discussion. In this activity, after reading an assignment, listening to a lecture, or viewing a video or DVD, students discuss a controversial central question about the topic, identify and consider possible alternative viewpoints to it, and then weigh these viewpoints. Then, in pairs, they discuss the pro and con alternatives they have identified, and come to a conclusion, recording all their thought processes on a graphic organizer. The Discussion Web strategy is especially effective because students must first reflect on the question individually and identify their own ideas about it, both pro and con. Next, they meet with a partner to share their lists of pro and con responses to the question. Once the lists have been shared, both students must reach a consensus as to which viewpoint they support, providing a single reason for their decision. This pair then joins another pair to share responses, repeating the process and reaching a group consensus on the question and supporting it with a single reason. Once all groups of four have reached consensus, they report their findings to the entire class. As always, the teacher should model this strategy for students before assigning it to them.

Steps for a Discussion Web

1. Provide each student with a text to read, a controversial question based on the reading to consider, and a copy of the Discussion Web graphic organizer.
2. Instruct students to consider both the pro and con sides of the question and list their responses in the appropriate sections of the graphic organizer. Stress that for every reason on the pro, or yes, side of the graphic organizer, they must provide a reason on the con, or no, side.
3. When students have completed their organizers individually, instruct them to pair with another student to compare their responses and discuss the evidence they have gathered for each alternative. Once they have completed their discussions, ask them to reach a consensus on the pro/con question and record it on the graphic organizer.
4. Next, ask each pair to join another pair of students to compare or discuss the evidence they have gathered for both sides of the

question. This group of four will now reach a consensus on the controversial question and, again, provide a single, best reason to support their decision. Remind them that if they do not agree on one conclusion, they must choose a conclusion most of them agree on.

5. Finally, ask one student from each group of four to present the group's consensus decision and reason for making their decision. (Note: To facilitate presentations, ask students to categorize all the reasons for their decision. Then allow the presenter to state only one support reason. If their first reason has been stated by another group, instruct the presenter to provide the "next best" reason: This gives students practice in prioritizing and eliminates the possibility that groups who report later in the class period will have no viable reasons left to share.

6. To bring personal closure to this activity as well as to help students reflect on how the Discussion Web strategy facilitated their learning, ask students to respond to the following questions:

   a. What conclusion did you personally come to?
   b. What is the best reason to support this conclusion?
   c. Did focusing on a question before you read help you understand the reading better?
   d. Did searching for evidence as you read help you understand the reading better?
   e. What was the most difficult step of the process? Why?
   f. Which step do you think best helped you understand? Explain.
   g. Did you change your mind about the question during any step of the process? Explain.

This strategy can be used in any content area. For example, in social studies, students can consider whether the death penalty should be repealed; in science, they can debate whether or not global warming is a danger to the environment; in English and language arts, they debate whether Hester Prynne should really have been condemned to wear the Scarlet Letter; and, finally, in health classes they can consider whether all children should be vaccinated in light of the suspected connection between some vaccines and autism. Figure 6.13 presents an example of a Discussion Web for English or language arts, while Figure 6.14 presents an example for science. Figure 6.27 at the end of the chapter provides a blackline master for this strategy.

Discussion Web for *No Promises in the Wind*

Position Statement: Josh was wrong to leave home.

1. Think about the position statement and fill in the graphic organizer.
2. For every YES reason you have, you must have a NO reason and vice versa.
3. Meet with your partner and compare/contrast the evidence you gave for each side of the question.
4. Reach consensus on whether you agree or disagree with the question, and choose ONE reason that best supports your decision.
5. Next, join another pair and reach consensus. Again, choose ONE reason that best supports your decision.
6. Report your decision to the class.

REASONS FOR		REASONS AGAINST
1. He traveled across the country and met many new people. 2. He learned that people can be different but still be okay. 3. He learned the power of love for others. 4. He learned the meaning of true friendship. 5. He learned to survive on his own. 6. He matured from his experience and finally began to understand his father.	**Reasons** **Question** Josh was wrong to leave home **Conclusion** Josh was right to leave home	1. He put himself and others in danger. 2. His little brother, Joey, was lost for many months. 3. His friend, Howie, was killed. 4. He left his family and worried them. 5. He could have died from the pneumonia he got.

What was your GROUP'S consensus? Josh should never have left home.

What was your PERSONAL opinion? It was okay for Josh to leave home; he grew up.

Looking at both sides of the question, what part of the Discussion Web process BEST helped you understand the selection?

Figure 6.13

Source: Based on Alvermann (1991).

Discussion Web for Genetic Engineering of Products

Position Statement: Products should not be genetically engineered.

1. Think about the position statement and fill in the graphic organizer.
2. For every YES reason you have, you must have a NO reason and vice versa.
3. Meet with your partner and compare/contrast the evidence you gave for each side of the question.
4. Reach consensus on whether you agree or disagree with the question, and choose ONE reason that best supports your decision.
5. Next, join another pair and reach consensus. Again, choose ONE reason that best supports your decision.
6. Report your decision to the class.

REASONS FOR

1. Scientists can develop more plentiful, nutritious foods.
2. Valuable traits from related species are combined to produce more valuable and productive crops and livestock.
3. It is a natural extension of traditional breeding.
4. Engineered plants and animals are thoroughly tested before being released into the food chain.
5. Engineered plants and animal foods are equivalent to other foods.
6. Engineered plants and animal foods have been sold for several years with no harmful effects found.
7. Some genetically engineered crops, like potatoes and corn, produce their own Bt, a pesticide that protects the crop from insects.

Reasons

Question
Products should not be genetically engineered

Conclusion
It is okay to genetically engineer products if they are well researched and tested.

REASONS AGAINST

1. It uses artificial laboratory techniques, which breach natural reproductive barriers.
2. It can disrupt natural genetic information encoded in DNA, causing unknown side effects.
3. Engineered products are tested only on animals, not on humans.
4. Little research in this area is reviewed by scientists or the FDA.
5. Engineered products are regulated as pesticides by the EPA.
6. Bt is a pesticide that people should not swallow, breathe, or get into open wounds.

What was your GROUP'S consensus? Genetic engineering is bad for use.

What was your PERSONAL opinion? Genetic engineering, if done safely, is okay.

What part of the Discussion Web process BEST helped you understand the selection? Trying to defend my position with my group.

Figure 6.14

Source: Based on Alvermann (1991).

REFLECTIONS

Again and again in this chapter, I have referred to the critical part reflection plays in a student's learning. Reflection enables students to look closely at what they are learning and thus helps them to monitor, assess, and, in turn, recognize how to improve their learning and thinking. In effect, they become metacognitively aware of their own thinking and learning processes. Furthermore, according to Fogarty, Perkins and Barell (1992), there seems to also be a direct connection between metacognitive reflection and the transfer of learning, and Moye (1997) declares that metacognition, in fact, leads to transfer. Thus, one cannot deny that helping students become metacognitive reflectors is crucial to helping them become independent, lifelong learners. In fact, as brain researchers tell us, it is during the transfer phase that connections are made and learning occurs. Reflective Lesson Log, 3-2-1, 1-2-3-4, Thinking at Right Angles, PMI, and What? So What? Now What? are all strategies that foster metacognitive reflection during the final stage of the lesson plan format.

Reflective Lesson Log

The Reflective Lesson Log (Burke, 2005) is an excellent way to introduce students to the critical thinking and reflection process so necessary to successful metacognitive transfer. This strategy encourages students to respond to what they have learned by taking time to write down the key ideas, connections, and questions they have encountered during their learning session. As Burke notes, "The students can use this time to think about the material, clarify confusion, discuss key ideas with group members, and process the information before the teacher moves on to the next segment of direct instruction" (p. 121).

Steps for the Reflective Lesson Log

1. After students have read, listened to a lecture, or viewed a movie or DVD, they write their responses to the following questions in a log:
   a. What are the key ideas from this lesson/discussion/reading?
   b. What connections can I make with other ideas?
   c. What questions do I still have?

2. Next, students share logs with a partner or group to discuss key ideas and answer any questions.

3. The teacher then conducts a discussion to answer any further questions or clarify any points.

4. Finally, the class discusses connections the students made between the information learned and other subject areas or life experiences.

5. The logs can be discussed the next day as a review of the previous day's learning.

As an added bonus, if students are absent, they can access the Reflective Lesson Logs of classmates and read them to catch up on the key ideas presented while they were not in school. See Figure 6.15 for an example of a Reflective Lesson Log for social studies and Figure 6.28 at the end of this chapter for a blackline master for this strategy.

Example of Reflective Lesson Log for Social Studies

Name _____ Date _____ Topic _____

What are the key ideas from this lesson/discussion/reading?

1. The land of Mesopotamia was formed in the valley between the Tigris and Euphrates rivers.
2. During the fourth millennium BCE, Mesopotamia became a great civilization.
3. It created a culture that lasted more than 3,000 years.
4. Ancient Mesopotamians had writing, cities, government, and literature, and they invented the wheel.
5. Sections of Mesopotamia were named Sumer, Akkad, Assyria, and Babylonia.
6. This area is now known as Iraq.

What connections can I make with other ideas?

I recognize the names of Babylonia and Assyria from stories I hear in Sunday School. I think Mesopotamia was the "Cradle of Civilization" that my Sunday School teacher talked about. Wow!

What questions do I still have?

Since the Mesopotamian civilization was so rich in culture and left so many artifacts, I wonder why the U.S. army did not protect the museum in Baghdad during the Iraq War to prevent looting and damage of the artifacts.

Figure 6.15

Source: Adapted from Burke (2005).

3-2-1 for Expository Text

The 3-2-1 strategy (Silver, Strong, & Perini, 2001) not only helps students reflect on what they have learned but also provides a brief summary for that learning and their reactions to it.

Steps for 3-2-1

1. After students have read, listened to a lecture, or viewed a video, they list the following on a piece of paper, index card, or in their learning journal:

   a. 3 facts, ideas, or concepts that really interested them

   b. 2 things they want to learn more about or have questions about

   c. 1 "big idea," which may be a concept or theme, they learned from today's lesson

2. Students then share their 3-2-1's with the class; this sets the stage for future discussion or instruction.

See Figure 6.16 for an example of 3-2-1 for mathematics and Figure 6.29 at the end of this chapter for a blackline master for this strategy.

Example of 3-2-1 for Mathematics

3-2-1 for Factors and Prime Factorization

3	1. A prime number is a whole number greater than 1 that has 2 factors. 2. A composite number is a whole number with more than 2 factors. 3. Prime factorization is when a composite number is written as a product of its prime factors.
2	1. Is the number 1 a prime or composite number? 2. How can I find the prime factors of a number?
1	1. I can find the prime factors of a number by using a factor tree.

Figure 6.16

3-2-1 for Narrative or Biographical Text

For narratives or biographies, Silver, Strong, and Perini (2001) suggest that students list

    a. 3 important facts in the character or person's life.

    b. 2 questions the students would ask the character or person if they could speak with her or him.

    c. 1 way the student is similar to or like the character or person.

Another one (1) question I often ask students when I use this strategy is, what connection can you make between the character or person and either you, another book you have read, or the world in general? As Keene and Zimmerman (1997) note, this helps students reflect on the relationship of the text to themselves, to other texts, and to the world and leads to better comprehension.

1-2-3-4 Strategy

The 1-2-3-4 strategy (Silver, Strong, & Perini, 2001) is similar to the 3-2-1 strategy discussed above and provides yet another way for students to employ their critical thinking to actively reflect upon their learning.

Steps for 1-2-3-4

1. After students have read, listened to a lecture, or viewed a video, they write their response to the following on a piece of paper or index card or in their learning journal:

    a. For the 1, students present the big idea that was learned.

    b. For the 2, students list as many details as they can to support the big idea.

    c. For the 3, students try to make as many personal connections to the topic as they can.

    d. For the 4, students pose any questions they might have about the content.

2. To conclude, students share their responses in pairs or small groups or with the entire class; this sharing then sets the stage for future discussion or instruction.

See Figure 6.17 for an example of 1-2-3-4 for English or language arts and Figure 6.30 at the end of this chapter for a blackline master for this strategy.

Example of 1-2-3-4 for English

1-2-3-4 for the Transcendentalism Period

1 Big Idea	Transcendentalism was a literary, political, and philosophical movement that occurred in America during the early nineteenth century.
2 Details to Support Big Idea	1. Members included Ralph Waldo Emerson, Henry David Thoreau, Margaret Fuller, Amos Bronson Alcott, Frederic Henry Hedge, and Theodore Parker. 2. This movement was similar to the Romanticism movement taking place in England and Germany. 3. The Transcendentalists were critical of their contemporary society because they felt it was too conformist. 4. Some Transcendalists like Thoreau and Emerson took solace in nature. 5. Transcendentalists developed social experiments like Brook Farm and Walden.
3 Personal Connections	I think the concern for global warming and the attempts to "think" green that are happening today come from the same thinking that the Transcendentalists had.
4 Questions You Still Have	1. Are there Transcendentalist writers today? 2. Do places like Brook Farm and Walden still exist?

Figure 6.17

Thinking at Right Angles

The Thinking at Right Angles strategy, as described in Burke (2005), encourages students to use critical thinking as well as both their cognitive and affective domains to reflect on what they have learned. In this strategy, students not only list the facts they have learned about a topic, but they also consider what feelings and associations they have about those facts, thereby addressing both the cognitive and affective domains.

Steps for Thinking at Right Angles

1. First, students write the name of the topic they have studied.
2. Next, they list as many facts about the topic as they can.
3. Then they record the feelings and associations they have in response to those facts.
4. Finally, they write a brief summary of their total learning experience.

See Figure 6.18 for an example of the Thinking at Right Angles strategy for mathematics and Figure 6.31 at the end of this chapter for a blackline master for it.

Example for Thinking at Right Angles for Mathematics: Rational Numbers

Name _____ Date _____ Topic <u>Writing fractions as decimals</u>

Directions: List the facts you learned about the topic in the **FACTS** section.
In the **FEELINGS** and **ASSOCIATIONS** section, write what you feel about and can associate with these facts.
Finally, in the **SUMMARY** section summarize what you have learned.

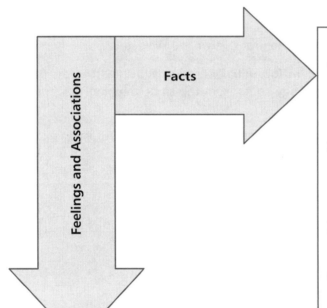

Feelings and Associations

Facts

Facts

1. Any rational number can be written as the quotient of two integers.
2. Any rational number can be written in decimal form by carrying out division.
3. If the remainder is 0, the decimal terminates.
4. If there is a remainder, the decimal repeats.

Feelings and Associations

1. Wow! I was really scared of doing this, but it helped to work with a partner to figure out some answers together.
2. We had to write down what we were doing step by step and write down where we had trouble. That helped me to ask questions later.
3. This was not so hard after all. Next we learn to write decimals as fractions. It should be easy!

Summary

1. I learned how to identify rational numbers.
2. To write a fraction as a decimal, I have to divide the denominator until the quotient terminates or repeats.

Figure 6.18

Source: Adapted from Burke (2005).

PMI

The PMI strategy (deBono, 1992) is similar to the well-known Plus/Delta strategy, but rather than just asking students to reflect on what was good or poor about a learning experience, this strategy takes students one step farther by asking them to utilize their critical thinking to evaluate that learning and then determine what impressed them as being intriguing or interesting about what they learned.

Steps for PMI

1. Ask students to list a PLUS or positive thing about their learning experience in the P section of the graphic organizer.
2. Ask students to list a MINUS or negative about their learning experience in the M section of the graphic organizer.
3. Ask students to list an interesting or intriguing thing about their learning experience in the I section of the graphic organizer.

See Figure 6.19 for an example of the PMI strategy for science or health and Figure 6.32 at the end of this chapter for a blackline master for the strategy.

Example of PMI for Science or Health

Name _____Topic_____ Date _____

Directions: After learning about your topic, complete the graphic organizer below.

P = List a **PLUS or POSITIVE** about what you learned; write it in the **Response/Idea** column. Explain why you thought it was a plus; write your explanation in the **Reflection/Why** column.

M= List a **MINUS or NEGATIVE** about what you learned; write it in the **Response/Idea** column. Explain why you thought it was a minus; write your explanation in the **Reflection/Why** column.

I = List an **INTERESTING or INTRIGUING** thing you learned; write it in the **Response/Idea** column. Explain why you thought it was interesting; write your explanation in the **Reflection/Why** column.

	Your Response (The Idea)	*Your Reflection (The Why)*
P	Many common diseases and their symptoms can often be prevented or alleviated with better nutrition.	Wow! Given what we now know about good eating, I could live to be 100 years old.
M	Many teens ignore what they learn about what constitutes good nutrition.	I often skip breakfast and eat snack food for lunch. I really should try to pay more attention to what I eat and when I eat it.
I	Teenage obesity could be prevented if more attention were paid to good nutritional habits.	I wonder why we have vending machines full of junk food in our school cafeteria.

Figure 6.19

What? So What? Now What?

One of the most powerful effects of using the What? So What? Now What? strategy (Silver, Strong, & Perini, 2001) for metacognitive transfer is that it not only encourages students to reflect on their learning but also encourages them to consider the implications of that learning.

Steps for What? So What? Now What?

1. **What:** In this step, students should consider what happened to them during the learning experience; what did they see? learn? feel? think?

2. **So What:** Next, students reflect on how what they observed, learned, or thought has made an impact on them. In other words, in this step, they consider how they have benefited from what they have seen, heard, and learned and how it has changed or added to their knowledge base.

3. **Now What:** In this step of the strategy students take their reflection one step further by considering what they will ultimately do with what they have seen, heard, or learned. In other words, how might they use their learning in other situations or how might they do things differently in the future as a result of what they have seen, heard, or learned?

See Figure 6.20 for an example of the What? So What? Now What? strategy for science or health and Figure 6.33 at the end of this chapter for a blackline master for this strategy.

Example of What? So What? Now What? for Science

What?	Methicillin-resistant Staphylococcus aureus (MRSA) infection is caused by Staphylococcus aureus bacteria, or "staph."
So What?	MRSA is resistant to the broad-spectrum antibiotics commonly used to treat it, so it can be fatal.
Now What?	I need to learn its symptoms and what to do in order to protect myself from getting MRSA.

Figure 6.20

CHAPTER SUMMARY

The final aspect of the block schedule lesson plan format is the Extend the Learner phase, and it asks students to clarify, reinforce, and extend what they have learned. In addition, it is during this stage that students organize the information they have gathered and use their critical thinking skills to synthesize, analyze, and evaluate it. Finally, this phase provides an opportunity for students to take time to reflect on their learning, which, in turn, enables them not only to clarify their learning but to focus their understanding as well, so they can better retain and act upon what they have learned. In fact, it is this process of metacognitive reflection that is so crucial to helping students become independent, lifelong learners.

The specific strategies that foster the critical thinking, metacognitive reflection, and independent thinking generated during this phase are presented in this chapter in six sections: (1) logs and journals, which includes the Double-Entry Journal; (2) conversations, which include Grand Conversations, Instructional Conversations, Poster Session, and Save the Last Word for Me; (3) extended format responses, which include Quickwrites, Quickdraws, and One Minute Papers; (4) creative after-learning strategies, which include Alphabet Catch, A to Z–Connect to Me, ABC Book, Biography Poem, Biography Cinquain, and RAFT; (5) employing different perspectives, which includes Corners, The Human Graph, Cubing, Perspective Cubing, and the Discussion Web; and (6) reflections, which includes the Reflective Lesson Log, 3-2-1, 1-2-3-4, Thinking at Right Angles, PMI, and What? So What? Now What?

BLACKLINE MASTERS

Blackline masters for implementing the strategies in this chapter may be found on pages 186 through 198.

Double-Entry Journal

Name _____ Topic _____ Date _____

Directions: As you read, note ideas, passages, or quotes that seem to stand out to you. They may surprise you, provide you with information you did not know before, or just make you think. Write them in Column 1 of the graphic organizer below. Write the page(s) where these ideas or quotes were found in Column 2. Then, in Column 3, record your response to what you read.

Key Ideas, Passages, or Quotes	Page Number	Feelings, Questions, and Concerns

Figure 6.21

Checklist for ABC Project
Excellent

Criteria	Self-Evaluation	Peer Evaluation	Teacher Evaluation
Topic selection is approved.			
Topic selection handed in on time.			
Rough draft approved.			
Rough draft handed in on time.			
Final story copy neatly done.			
Assignment rules followed accurately, completely.			
Illustrations creatively done.			
Project completed on time.			

Good

Criteria	Self-Evaluation	Peer Evaluation	Teacher Evaluation
Topic selection is approved.			
Topic selection handed in late.			
Rough draft approved.			
Rough draft handed in late.			
Final story copy neatly done.			
Assignment rules followed accurately, completely.			
Illustrations generally creative.			
Final project not completed on time.			

Incomplete

Criteria	Self-Evaluation	Peer Evaluation	Teacher Evaluation
Topic selection not approved.			
Topic selection handed in late.			
Rough draft not completed or not approved.			
Final story copy poorly done with errors, messy.			
Final story copy neatly done.			
Assignment rules not followed.			
Illustrations lack creativity.			
Final project not completed on time.			

Figure 6.22

Biography Poem

Directions: Think about what makes your topic special. Make a list of words to describe the topic. Then, using the recipe below, use these words to make up a poem about your topic. You may want to illustrate your poem with a picture or photograph or play music as you read your poem.

Topic: _____

Four traits to describe the topic:	
Relative of:	
Lover of (list three things):	
Who feels (list three items):	
Who needs (list three items):	
Who fears (list three items):	
Who gives (list three items):	
Who would like to see (list three items):	
Resident of:	
Last name for topic:	

Figure 6.23

Source: From *Reading and Writing Across Content Areas* (2nd ed., p. 182), by R. L. Sejnost and S. Thiese, 2007, Thousand Oaks, CA: Corwin. Copyright © 2007 by Corwin. Reprinted with permission.

Biography Cinquain

Directions: Think about what makes your topic special. Make a list of words to describe the topic. Then, using the recipe below, use these words to make up a poem about your topic. You may want to illustrate your poem with a picture or photograph or play music as you read your poem.

Topic: _____

Name the topic:	
Two adjectives to describe the topic:	
Three verbs or adverbs to describe the topic:	
Two more adjectives to describe the topic, or a description of the topic:	
State the topic again:	

Figure 6.24

Creating a Cube

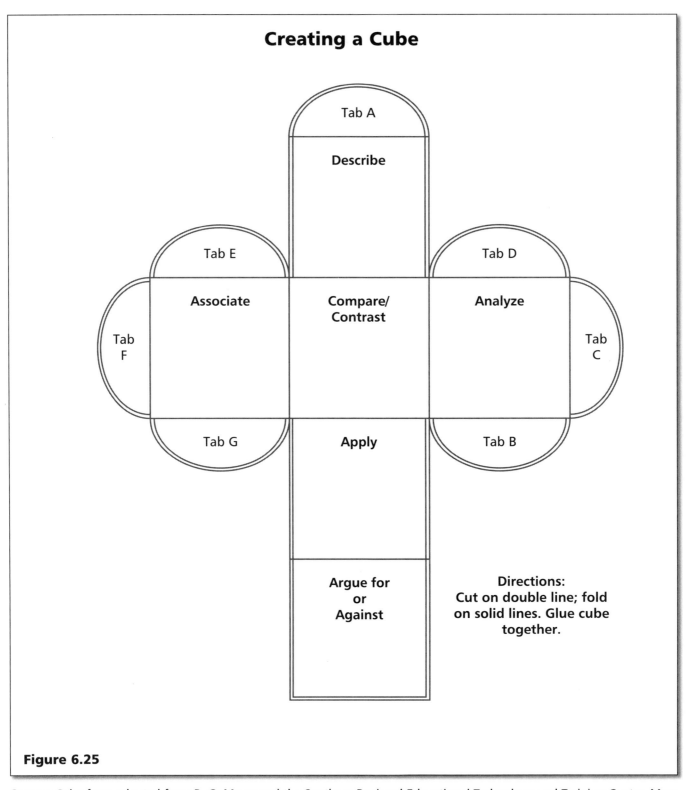

Figure 6.25

Source: Cube form adapted from R. G. Meyer and the Southern Regional Educational Technology and Training Center, Mays Landing, New Jersey.

Cube Diagram

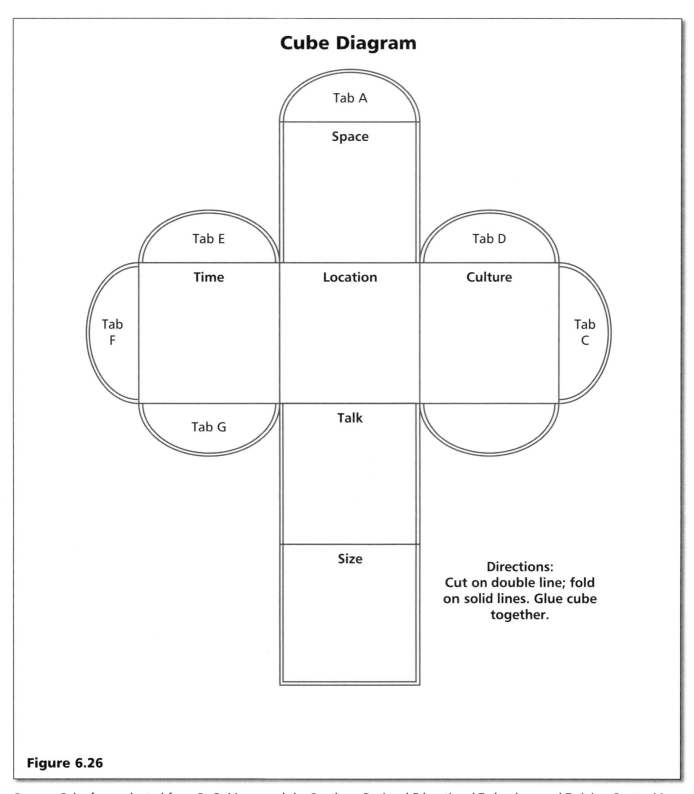

Figure 6.26

Source: Cube form adapted from R. G. Meyer and the Southern Regional Educational Technology and Training Center, Mays Landing, New Jersey.

Discussion Web

1. Think about the position statement and fill in the graphic organizer.

2. For every YES reason you have, you must have a NO reason and vice versa.

3. Meet with your partner and compare/contrast the evidence you gave for each side of the statement.

4. Reach consensus on whether you agree or disagree with the statement and choose ONE reason that best supports your decision.

5. Next, join another pair and reach consensus. Again, choose ONE reason that best supports your decision.

6. Report your decision to the class.

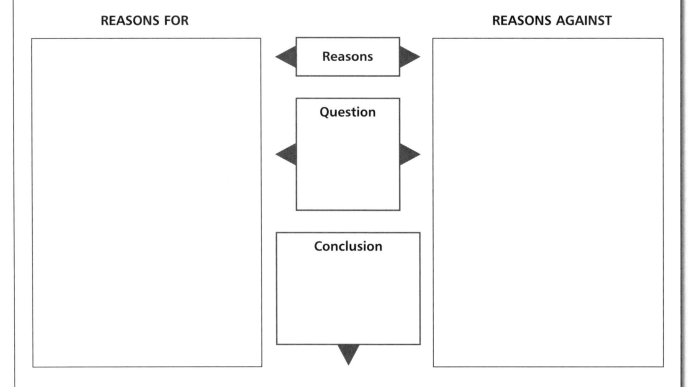

REASONS FOR   **REASONS AGAINST**

Reasons

Question

Conclusion

What was your GROUP'S consensus?

What was your PERSONAL opinion?

What part of the Discussion Web process BEST helped you understand the selection?

Figure 6.27

Source: Adapted from Alvermann (1991).

Reflective Lesson Log

Name _____ Date _____ Topic _____

After studying your topic, complete the graphic organizer by listing

- the key ideas you learned in this segment.
- what connection you make with other ideas.
- what questions you still have about the topic.

What are the key ideas from this lesson/discussion/reading?

What connections can I make with other ideas?

What questions do I still have?

Figure 6.28

3-2-1

Name _____ Date _____ Topic _____

After studying your topic, complete the graphic organizer by listing

- 3 facts, ideas, or concepts that really interested you.
- 2 things you want to learn more about or have questions about.
- 1 "big idea" you learned from today's study.

3	
2	
1	

Figure 6.29

1-2-3-4

Name _____ Date _____ Topic _____

After studying your topic, complete the graphic organizer by listing

    1. the "big idea" you learned from today's study.

    2. details to support the "big idea"—3 facts, ideas, or concepts that really interested you.

    3. personal connections to the topic you can make.

    4. any questions you might have about the content.

1	
2	
3	
4	

Figure 6.30

Thinking at Right Angles

Name _____ Date _____ Topic _____

Directions: List the facts you learned about the topic in the **FACTS** section.
In the **FEELINGS** and **ASSOCIATIONS** section, write what you feel
about and can associate with these facts.
Finally, in the **SUMMARY** section summarize what you have learned.

Facts

Feelings and Associations

Facts

Feelings and Associations

Summary

Figure 6.31

Source: Adapted from Burke (2005).

PMI

Name _____ **Topic** _____ **Date** _____

Directions: After learning about your topic, complete the graphic organizer below.

P = List a **PLUS or POSITIVE** about what you learned; write it in the **Response/Idea** column. Explain why you thought it was a plus; write your response in the **Reflection/Why** column.

M= List a **MINUS or NEGATIVE** about you learned; write it in the **Response/Idea** column. Explain why you thought it was a minus; write your response in the **Reflection/Why** column.

I = List an **INTERESTING** or **INTRIGUING** thing you learned about; write it in the **Response/Idea** column. Explain why you thought it was interesting; write your response in the **Reflection/Why** column.

	Your Response (The Idea)	*Your Reflection (The Why)*
P		
M		
I		

Figure 6.32

What? So What? Now What?

Name_____Topic_____Date _____

Directions: After studying your topic, complete the graphic organizer by writing

- what you learned in the WHAT column.

- how that learning has impacted you in the SO WHAT column.

- an explanation of what you need to do as a result of what you have learned in the NOW WHAT column.

What?	
So What?	
Now What?	

Figure 6.33

CHAPTER 7

Enact the Learning

One must learn by doing the thing; for though you think you know it, you have no certainty, until you try.

—Sophocles

THE CULMINATION: ENACTMENT

This book was written on the premise that the use of block scheduling in the middle school and high school classrooms of today is both valid and valuable for students. In essence, a myriad of researchers have shown that extending the length of class time for students, especially adolescents, provides many benefits, for when students attend class for a time period longer than the usual 45 or 50 minutes, they have both the time and the opportunity to

- get to know their teachers and classmates better.
- study concepts in greater depth.
- engage in hands-on and laboratory activities that focus on in-depth learning experiences.
- participate in cooperative learning groups.
- take advantage of accommodations for their individual learning styles and the need for extensive practice if needed.
- engage in prolonged inquiry and discussion.
- utilize technology effectively.

Unfortunately, as noted earlier, the task of teaching in an extended time period sometimes causes apprehension among middle and secondary school teachers as they struggle with how to keep their students actively engaged in learning for 90 to 100 minutes. Many times teachers merely lecture longer and have students take notes and then engage in busy work or begin their homework to fill the remainder of the extended class period time. However, in the fast-paced world of today's adolescence, this strategy simply does not work.

What, then, can the teacher who teaches in a school that follows a block schedule format do? This book is my attempt to answer that question by providing suggestions for curriculum planning and presenting some basic teaching techniques to use in the classroom, such as brain-based learning, cooperative learning, the use of multiple intelligences theory, effective questioning techniques, and graphic organizers. The book presents a lesson plan format to deliver classroom instruction within the 90 minute block of time and describes a variety of instructional strategies and activities that lend themselves to enticing, enlightening, engaging, and extending the adolescent learner.

The lesson plan, detailed in chapters 3, 4, 5, and 6 of this book, consists of a four-pronged format. The first phase, Entice the Learner, lasts approximately 10 to 15 minutes; the second phase, Enlighten the Learner, lasts approximately 15 to 20 minutes; the third phase, Engage the Learner, lasts approximately 20 to 30 minutes; and the fourth phase, Extend the Learner, lasts approximately 20 to 30 minutes. This final chapter of this book, Enact the Learning, provides specific lesson plan examples that utilize the research-based strategies and activities discussed throughout the text.

STRATEGIES AND ACTIVITIES TO USE IN EACH PHASE OF THE LESSON PLAN FORMAT

Figure 7.1 provides a summary of the phases of the lesson plan format presented in this book as well as the instructional strategies and activities that are appropriate for each phase, so it is clear when and where and how to use them. In addition, specific lesson ideas for a variety of content area subjects are detailed in Figures 7.2 through 7.10. In each of the lesson ideas provided, if an example of the strategy relates directly to the lesson's content discipline, it is denoted as a specific example, while if the example relates to another content discipline, it is denoted as an illustration.

Strategies and Activities to
Use During the Steps of
the Block Schedule Lesson Format

Entice the Learner Phase: Approximately 10 to 15 minutes

1. Brain Writing
2. Carousel Brainstorming
3. Exclusion Brainstorming
4. Think-Pair-Share
5. Think-Pair-Share Variation
6. Three Step Interview
7. Hooks and Bridges
8. Mind's Eye
9. Story Impressions
10. Problematic Perspectives
11. Character Quotes
12. Anticipation Guide
13. True or False
14. Knowledge Rating
15. Possible Sentences

Enlighten the Learner Phase: Approximately 15 to 20 minutes

1. Teacher modeling
2. Teacher and student demonstrations, simulations, or laboratories
3. Guest speakers
4. Small or whole group discussions
5. Text Jigsaw
6. Reciprocal Questioning
7. Socratic Seminars
8. Direct instruction of a minilesson
9. Audio presentations/videotapes/CD-ROM presentations
10. Say Something
11. Write a Question
12. Press Conference
13. Exam Questions
14. Concrete Images
15. Picture Making
16. Paired Discussions
17. Send a Problem
18. Learning Stations

(Continued)

(Continued)

Engage the Learner Phase: Approximately 20 to 30 minutes

1. Reciprocal Teaching
2. Question-Answer Relationship Strategy (QARS)
3. Questioning the Author
4. ReQuest
5. Socratic Questioning
6. Structured Note Taking
7. Learning Stations
8. SMART
9. INSERT
10. Guided Note Taking
11. Reader's Questions
12. 5W Model
13. Extended Anticipation Guide
14. About/Point
15. Magnet Summaries
16. Sketch to Stretch
17. Jot Charts
18. Pyramid Diagram
19. Three Level Guide

Extend the Learner Phase: Approximately 20 to 25 minutes

1. Double-Entry Journal
2. Grand Conversations
3. Instructional Conversations
4. Poster Session
5. Save the Last Word for Me
6. Quickwrites
7. Quickdraws
8. One Minute Papers
9. Alphabet Catch
10. A to Z–Connect to Me
11. ABC Alphabet Book
12. Biography Poem
13. Biography Cinquain
14. Fact Acrostic

15. RAFT

16. Corners

17. The Human Graph

18. Cubing

19. Perspective Cubing

20. Discussion Web

21. Reflective Lesson Log

22. 3-2-1 for Expository Text

23. 1-2-3-4 for Narrative or Biographical Text

24. Thinking at Right Angles

25. PMI

26. What? So What? Now What?

Figure 7.1

LESSON IDEAS FOR CONTENT AREA DISCIPLINES

Lesson Idea for English

The focus of this lesson is on beginning a study of the novel, *The Light in the Forest,* by Conrad Richter. During the enticement stage of the lesson plan, students will begin their study by completing the Problematic Perspectives strategy, a specific example of which can be found in Chapter 3, Figure 3.13, and continue into the enlightenment stage of the lesson by jigsawing Chapter 1 of the novel and developing a set of questions to discuss based on the Press Conference strategy discussed in Chapter 4 of this book. During the engagement phase, students will complete a 5W model graphic organizer as discussed in Chapter 5, and will conclude with the final extension stage by participating in small group discussions that revolve around statements chosen from the novel through the use of the Save the Last Word for Me strategy discussed in Chapter 6.

Lesson Idea for English
One Day Lesson Plan Template for English

Consult the standards and list those that can be addressed in the unit.

As you plan your lesson, consider what teaching and learning experiences will equip students to demonstrate the targeted understandings.

- What will students need to know or understand as a result of this lesson?
- What will students be able to do as a result of this lesson?
- What assessments will show what students know and are able to do?

Topic: *The Light in the Forest,* Chapter 1

Step	Time	Strategies	Assessment
Entice the Learner	Suggested time: 10–15 minutes	Problematic Perspectives (See Chapter 3, Figure 3.13 for a specific example.)	Class sharing of answers in small groups
Objectives	Suggested time: 3–5 minutes	Use questions and predictions to guide reading across complex materials. Summarize and make generalizations from content and relate to the purpose of the material. Describe the influence of the author's language structure and word choice to convey the author's viewpoint.	
Enlighten the Learner	Suggested time: 15–20 minutes	Jigsaw of Chapter 1; Press Conference strategy (See Chapter 4)	Completion of Press Conference questions
Engage the Learner	Suggested time: 20–30 minutes	5W Model graphic organizer on Chapter 1 (See Chapter 5, Figure 5.7 for an illustration and Figure 5.19 for a blackline master for the strategy.)	Completion of 5W Model
Extend the Learner	Suggested time: 20–25 minutes	In small groups, students participate in the Save the Last Word for Me strategy. (See Chapter 6 for details.)	Discussion of statements chosen for Save the Last Word for Me strategy

Figure 7.2

Lesson Idea for Language Arts

The language arts lesson in Figure 7.3 presents a balanced literacy approach to teaching that includes word work or vocabulary, shared reading, guided reading, independent and shared writing, guided writing, and independent writing.

Week-Long Language Arts/Literature Lesson Plan

Name: Tricia Teacher

Week of: October 15, 2007

Desired Results of Unit: Students will apply inference strategies when reading, practice narrative writing, and increase vocabulary.

Knowledge and Skills Needed: Students will need to know how to communicate, listen, read independently, and write.

State Standards: 1. read with understanding 2. read literature from different perspectives 3. write for a variety of purposes 4. listen and speak effectively for different purposes

Themes/Questions: How do our choices and their consequences shape our lives?

	Monday	Tuesday	Wednesday	Thursday	Friday
Entice the Learner *Warm-Up:* 10 minutes	Test Taking Tips article and questions Independent	The Armadillo ISAT practice Independent	Map It! critical thinking worksheet Partners	Journal Question critical thinking Independent	Ferris Wheel Fun word work Independent
Enlighten the Learner *Read/Think Aloud* 20 minutes	Anthology—*Flowers for Algernon*—introduce text with focus on *inferring* Whole Class				
Enlighten the Learner *Shared Reading* 20 minutes		*Flowers*-continue reading text, stopping at points to discuss *inferences*—Whole Class/Partners			
Engage the Learner *Guided Reading Groups* 20 minutes per group		A. *Dogs Don't Tell Jokes* Share inferences from Ch. 3; preview Ch. 4&5 assign inference WS B. *Among the Hidden* Review inference WS Begin reading Ch. 6 Assign 6&7 Small Groups	C. *Stuck in Neutral* Share character inferences from Ch. 2 Assign Ch. 3&4 D. *Romeo & Juliet* Review inference WS with group Assign Ch. 11–13 Small Groups	A. *Dogs* Review inference WS Ch. 6&7 record inferences in journal B. *Hidden* Discuss inferences from Ch. 6&7 Assign Ch. 8&9 with WS Small Groups	C. *Neutral* Review character inferences w. evidence. Preview Ch. 4 Assign Ch. 5&6 D. *R&J* Discuss inferences made in Ch. 11–13. Assign Ch. 14 Small Groups

(Continued)

(Continued)

Engage the Learner *Independent Reading* **20 minutes**	Collect reading logs from previous week. Read for reading log. Independent	Read for reading log Teacher conferences with 4 students Independent	Read for reading log Teacher conferences with 4 students Independent	*Flowers* vocabulary quiz Independent	Read for reading log Teacher conferences with 4 students Independent
Engage the Learner *Word Work/ Vocabulary* **20 minutes**	*Flowers*—draw definitions for vocabulary words. Due Wed. Independent	Review vocabulary from *Flowers* Partners	Collect vocabulary work. Study words for quiz with a partner	Spelling practice Independent	
Engage the Learner *Spelling* **15 (20) minutes**		Pretest list Independent	Spelling practice Independent	Writing sentences grammar book Ch. 8 pp. 269–272 Whole Class	Spelling test Whole Class
Engage the Learner *Writing Minilesson* **15 (20) minutes**		Openings for narrative essays Whole Class			Assign WB 17 on sentences; review answers together Independent/ Whole Class
Extend the Learner *Writing: 20 minutes Shared, Guided Independent*	Narrative essays Brainstorm ideas related to *Algernon* theme Whole Class	Draft opening for narrative related to *Algernon* theme Independent	Share openings Continue to work on essay Whole Class/ Independent		Continue work on narrative essay Independent

Figure 7.3

Source: Developed by Cynthia Bolanowski, Literacy Consultant, Kane County Regional Office of Education, Geneva, Illinois.

Lesson Idea for Science

The focus of the science lesson is a continuation of the study of plant and animal cells. In the enticement stage of the lesson plan, students participate in the True or False strategy discussed in Chapter 3 to help them review material already learned about plant and animal cells. Next, during the enlightenment stage, they view a CD-ROM to further reinforce previous learning. After viewing the CD-ROM, students enter the engagement stage by moving through three multiple intelligence–based learning stations, a specific example of which can be found in Chapter 4, to cement their knowledge of plant and animals cells. Finally, in the extension stage, all students participate in the fourth learning station to reflect on their learning; a detailed example of this kind of learning station can be found in Figure 4.2.

Lesson Idea for Science
One Day Lesson Plan Template for Science

Consult the standards and list those that can be addressed in the unit.

As you plan your lesson, consider what teaching and learning experiences will equip students to demonstrate the targeted understandings.

- What will students need to know or understand as a result of this lesson?
- What will students be able to do as a result of this lesson?
- What assessments will show what students know and are able to do?

Topic: Plant and Animal Cells

Step	Time	Strategies	Assessment
Entice the Learner	Suggested time: 10–15 minutes	True or False strategy on plant and animal cells (See Chapter 3.)	Class sharing of answers
Objectives	Suggested time: 3–5 minutes	• Understand all living things are composed of cells: small parts that function similarly in all living things. Understand that different tissues have different, specialized cells with specific functions. Understand the levels of organization in living organism: cells, tissues, organs, and organ systems. • Identify the main differences between plant cells and animal cells, namely that plant cells have chloroplasts and cell walls (which provide rigidity to the plant, since plants have no skeletons). Identify the basic cell organelles and their functions.	

(Continued)

(Continued)

Step	Time	Strategies	Assessment
Enlighten the Learner	Suggested time: 15–20 minutes	CD-ROM presentation to review plant and animal cells	Successful completion of Learning Station activities
Engage the Learner	Suggested time: 20–30 minutes	Begin Learning Station rotation: Learning Station 1: Let's Question, using the verbal/linguistic intelligence Learning Station 2: Everybody Looks, using the visual/spatial intelligence Learning Station 3: Look Like a Cell, using the bodily/kinesthetic and interpersonal intelligences	Successful completion of Learning Station activities
Extend the Learner	Suggested time: 20–25 minutes	Begin Learning Station 4: Students create a foldable booklet that synthesizes their knowledge of the two types of cells through a compare/contrast list. See Chapter 4, Figure 4.2.	Successful creation of pamphlet

Figure 7.4

Lesson Idea for Social Studies

This social studies lesson is a continuation of a lesson on the Industrial Revolution. In the enticement phase, students complete the Possible Sentences strategy, a specific example of which can be found in Chapter 3, Figure 3.23, and continue into the enlightenment stage of the lesson by listening to an Interactive Lecture and then using the Pair Discussions strategy, both of which are discussed in Chapter 4. In the engagement phase of the lesson plan, students complete the Reader's Questions graphic organizer discussed in Chapter 5. The lesson will conclude with students completing the Cubing strategy discussed in Chapter 6.

Lesson Idea for Social Studies
One Day Lesson Plan Template for Social Studies

Consult the standards and list those that can be addressed in the unit.

As you plan your lesson, consider what teaching and learning experiences will equip students to demonstrate the targeted understandings.

- What will students need to know or understand as a result of this lesson?
- What will students be able to do as a result of this lesson?
- What assessments will show what students know and are able to do?

Topic: The Industrial Revolution

Step	Time	Strategies	Assessment
Entice the Learner	Suggested time: 10–15 minutes	Possible Sentences (See Chapter 3, Figure 3.23 for a specific example of this strategy.)	Class sharing of answers in small groups
Objectives	Suggested time: 3–5 minutes	• Explain the relationships among the American economy and slavery, immigration, industrialization, and urbanization. • Explain how market prices signal producers about what, how, and how much to produce. • Explain the relationship between productivity and wages.	
Enlighten the Learner	Suggested time: 15–20 minutes	Interactive Lecture on pages 198–220 in the text with Paired Discussions (See Chapter 4 for details.)	Completion of Paired Discussions
Engage the Learner	Suggested time: 20–30 minutes	About/Point strategy (See Chapter 5, figures 5.9 and 5.10 for illustrations and Figure 5.19 for a blackline master for the strategy.)	Completion of Reader's Questions graphic organizer
Extend the Learner	Suggested time: 20–25 minutes	Cubing strategy (See Chapter 6, Figure 6.11 for an illustration and Figure 6.25 for a blackline master for the strategy.)	Oral presentation of Cubing assignment

Figure 7.5

Lesson Idea for Mathematics

The focus of this math lesson is on introducing polygons. Students begin the enticement phase by completing an anticipation guide on polygons, a specific example of which can be seen in Chapter 3, Figure 3.17, and then move into the enlightenment phase by joining the teacher and other students in a demonstration of polygons based on text information. Next, during the engagement phase, students write a Magnet Summary, discussed in Chapter 5, detailing the essential information about polygons. The lesson ends with the students working in small groups to develop a Fact Acrostic, discussed in Chapter 6, on polygons.

Lesson Idea for Mathematics
One Day Lesson Plan Template for Mathematics

Consult the standards and list those that can be addressed in the unit.

As you plan your lesson, consider what teaching and learning experiences will equip students to demonstrate the targeted understandings.

- What will students need to know or understand as a result of this lesson?
- What will students be able to do as a result of this lesson?
- What assessments will show what students know and are able to do?

Topic: Polygons

Step	Time	Strategies	Assessment
Entice the Learner	Suggested time: 10–15 minutes	Anticipation Guide for polygons (See Chapter 3, Figure 3.17, for a specific example of the strategy.)	Class sharing of answers in small groups
Objectives	Suggested time: 3–5 minutes	• Identify, sketch, label, and describe the properties of geometric figures. • Use geometric figures and their properties to solve problems.	
Enlighten the Learner	Suggested time: 15–20 minutes	Teacher modeling and student demonstrations of polygons based on text, pages 79–85 (See Chapter 4 for details.)	Development of Magnet Summary explaining polygons
Engage the Learner	Suggested time: 20–30 minutes	Magnet Summary of essential information about polygons (See Chapter 5, Figure 5.11 for an illustration and Figure 5.20 for a blackline master of the strategy.)	Completion of Magnet Summary
Extend the Learner	Suggested time: 20–25 minutes	RAFT assignment (See Chapter 6, figures 6.9 and 6.10 for illustrations of the strategy.) **Role:** Specific polygon (student chooses one) **Audience:** Circle **Format:** Resume **Topic:** Presenting attributes, experiences, and abilities of the chosen polygon	Completion of RAFT assignment

Figure 7.6

Lesson Idea for Health

This health lesson continues the study of how to prevent diseases by focusing on the topic of bacteria. During the enticement phase, students conduct a Three Step Interview, discussed in Chapter 3, and, during the enlightenment phase, students listen to a lecture on bacteria presented by the school nurse. After listening to the guest speaker, students move into the engagement phase and complete a Three Level Guide on bacteria (a specific example of a Three Level Guide can be found in Chapter 5, Figure 5.16) and complete the lesson during the extension phase by developing a Quickwrite, discussed in Chapter 6.

Lesson Idea for Health
One Day Lesson Plan Template for Health

Consult the standards and list those that can be addressed in the unit.

As you plan your lesson, consider what teaching and learning experiences will equip students to demonstrate the targeted understandings.

- What will students need to know or understand as a result of this lesson?
- What will students be able to do as a result of this lesson?
- What assessments will show what students know and are able to do?

Topic: Bacteria

Step	Time	Strategies	Assessment
Entice the Learner	Suggested time: 10–15 minutes	Three Step Interview on bacteria (See Chapter 3, Figure 3.6 for an illustration of this strategy.)	Class sharing of answers in small groups
Objectives	Suggested time: 3–5 minutes	• Compare and contrast communicable illnesses. • Analyze the possible outcomes of effective illness prevention.	
Enlighten the Learner	Suggested time: 15–20 minutes	Guest Speaker, school nurse	Student participation in question and answer period following speaker
Engage the Learner	Suggested time: 20–30 minutes	Three Level Guide on bacteria (See Chapter 5, Figure 5.16 for a specific example of the strategy.)	Completion of Three Level Guide
Extend the Learner	Suggested time: 20–25 minutes	Quickwrite on bacteria (See Chapter 6, Figure 6.2 for an illustration of the strategy.)	Completion of Quickwrite assignment

Figure 7.7

Lesson Idea for Family and Consumer Education

In order to begin the study of nutrition, this family and consumer science lesson focuses on identifying the properties of fats, carbohydrates, nucleic acids, and proteins. During the enticement phase, students engage in the Give One–Get One illustrated in Chapter 3 and validate their knowledge during the enlightenment phase as the teacher presents a minilesson on the topic. Finally, during the engagement phase, students complete a Jot Chart, a specific example of which can be seen in Chapter 5, Figure 5.13, to record their newly gained knowledge; and in the extension phase, they create a Fact Acrostic, discussed in Chapter 6, to share their knowledge with their classmates.

Lesson Idea for Family and Consumer Science

One Day Lesson Plan Template for Family and Consumer Science

Consult the standards and list those that can be addressed in the unit.

As you plan your lesson, consider what teaching and learning experiences will equip students to demonstrate the targeted understandings.

- What will students need to know or understand as a result of this lesson?
- What will students be able to do as a result of this lesson?
- What assessments will show what students know and are able to do?

Topic: Fats, Carbohydrates, Nucleic Acids, and Proteins

Step	Time	Strategies	Assessment
Entice the Learner	Suggested time: 10–15 minutes	Give One–Get One strategy on fats, carbohydrates, nucleic acids, and proteins (See Chapter 3, Figure 3.5 for an illustration of this strategy.)	Class sharing of answers in small groups
Objectives	Suggested time: 3–5 minutes	• Explain how body system functions can be maintained and improved through nutrition. • Explain immediate and long-term effects of diet on the body systems (e.g. diet/heart).	
Enlighten the Learner	Suggested time: 15–20 minutes	Minilesson on fats, carbohydrates, nucleic acids, and proteins	Student participation in question and answer period following minilesson
Engage the Learner	Suggested time: 20–30 minutes	Jot Chart on fats, carbohydrates, nucleic acids, and proteins (See Chapter 5, Figure 5.13 for a specific example of the strategy.)	Completion of Jot Chart
Extend the Learner	Suggested time: 20–25 minutes	Fact Acrostic on one of the following: fats, carbohydrates, nucleic acids, or proteins (See Chapter 6, figures 6.7 and 6.8 for illustrations of the strategy.)	Completion of Fact Acrostic assignment

Figure 7.8

Lesson Idea for Business and Technology

This business/technology lesson introduces students to the basics needed to properly operate a computer. Students utilize the Think-Pair-Share strategy during the enticement phase of the lesson to foster their prior knowledge of the topic. Next, during the enlightenment phase, the teacher presents an interactive demonstration of the elements of a computer, and the students will complete a Guided Note Taking worksheet during their engagement phase (see Chapter 5 for a discussion of this strategy). Finally, they extend their learning by creating a Biography Cinquain on computers, a specific example of which can be found in Chapter 6, Figure 6.6.

Lesson Idea for Business and Technology

One Day Lesson Plan Template for Business and Technology

Consult the standards and list those that can be addressed in the unit.

As you plan your lesson, consider what teaching and learning experiences will equip students to demonstrate the targeted understandings.

- What will students need to know or understand as a result of this lesson?
- What will students be able to do as a result of this lesson?
- What assessments will show what students know and are able to do?

Topic: Introduction to Computers

Step	Time	Strategies	Assessment
Entice the Learner	Suggested time: 10–15 minutes	Think-Pair-Share on topic of computers (See Chapter 3 for a discussion of the strategy.)	Class sharing of answers in small groups
Objectives	Suggested time: 3–5 minutes	• Identify the hardware options in available current technology. • Locate and identify the specific parts of a computer. • Understand how to successfully boot a computer.	
Enlighten the Learner	Suggested time: 15–20 minutes	Teacher demonstration of elements of a computer	Student participation in question and answer period following speaker
Engage the Learner	Suggested time: 20–30 minutes	Guided Note Taking on elements of the computer (See Chapter 5, figures 5.3 and 5.4 for illustrations of the strategy.)	Completion of Guided Note Taking
Extend the Learner	Suggested time: 20–25 minutes	Biography Cinquain on computers (the Internet) (See Chapter 6, Figure 6.6 for a specific example and Figure 6.24 for a blackline master for the strategy.)	Completion of Biography Cinquain assignment

Figure 7.9

Lesson Idea for Foreign Language

The foreign language lesson provides students with an in-depth look at the artists Frida Kahlo and her husband, Diego Rivera. The enticement phase introduces the students to the two artists through the use of the Character Quotes strategy, discussed in Chapter 3. Next, during the enlightenment phase, students view Part 1 of the video *Frida Kahlo* and complete the Say Something strategy discussed in Chapter 4. After viewing the video and discussing what they saw, students will move into the engagement phase by completing the Reader's Questions graphic organizer, discussed in Chapter 5. Finally, they extend their learning by creating a Biography Poem, a specific example of which can be found in Chapter 6, Figure 6.5.

Lesson Idea for Foreign Language

One Day Lesson Plan Template for Foreign Language

Consult the standards and list those that can be addressed in the unit.

As you plan your lesson, consider what teaching and learning experiences will equip students to demonstrate the targeted understandings.

- What will students need to know or understand as a result of this lesson?
- What will students be able to do as a result of this lesson?
- What assessments will show what students know and are able to do?

Topic: Frida Kahlo and Diego Rivera

Step	Time	Strategies	Assessment
Entice the Learner	Suggested time: 10–15 minutes	Character Quotes for Frida Kahlo and Diego Rivera (See Chapter 3, figures 3.14 and 3.15 for illustrations of this strategy.)	Class sharing of quote analysis in small groups
Objectives	Suggested time: 3–5 minutes	• Identify key historical figures and events associated with areas where the target language is spoken and explain their influence. • Compare and contrast the influences of historical figures and events and their impact on the development of their countries.	
Enlighten the Learner	Suggested time: 15–20 minutes	Video presentation, *Frida Kahlo*, Part 1, and Say Something strategy (See Chapter 4.)	Completion of Say Something Discussions
Engage the Learner	Suggested time: 20–30 minutes	Reader's Questions prepared on Part 1 of video (See Chapter 5, figures 5.5 and 5.6 for an illustration and Figure 5.17 for a blackline master for the strategy.)	Completion of Reader's Questions
Extend the Learner	Suggested time: 20–25 minutes	Biography Poem on Frida Kahlo (See Chapter 6, Figure 6.5 for a specific example and Figure 6.23 for a blackline master for the strategy.)	Completion of Biography Poem assignment

Figure 7.10

Lesson Idea for Fine Arts

The focus of this fine arts lesson revolves around the study of Mozart and his music. To entice the students, the teacher conducts a Brain Writing activity, discussed in Chapter 3, so students can share what they may already know about the topic. Next, the teacher plays a collection of Mozart's musical compositions for the students, and students complete the Picture Making activity, discussed in Chapter 4. As the lesson progresses, students engage in completing a Reader's Questions graphic organizer, a specific example of which is provided in Chapter 5, Figure 5.6, and extend their learning by reflecting on what they have learned in a Reflective Lesson Log, discussed in Chapter 6.

Lesson Idea for Fine Arts

One Day Lesson Plan Template for Fine Arts

Consult the standards and list those that can be addressed in the unit.

As you plan your lesson, consider what teaching and learning experiences will equip students to demonstrate the targeted understandings.

- What will students need to know or understand as a result of this lesson?
- What will students be able to do as a result of this lesson?
- What assessments will show what students know and are able to do?

Topic: The Music of Mozart

Step	Time	Strategies	Assessment
Entice the Learner	Suggested time: 10–15 minutes	Brain Writing strategy (See Chapter 3, Figure 3.1 for an illustration of the strategy.)	Class sharing of answers in small groups
Objectives	Suggested time: 3–5 minutes	• Analyze and classify the distinguishing characteristics of historical music by style, period, and culture. • Analyze how the arts shape and reflect ideas, issues, or themes in a particular culture or historical period.	
Enlighten the Learner	Suggested time: 15–20 minutes	Teacher demonstration of music written by Mozart and Picture Making strategy (See Chapter 4 for details.)	Sharing of pictures created while listening to the music
Engage the Learner	Suggested time: 20–30 minutes	Reader's Questions (See Chapter 5, Figure 5.6, for a specific example and Figure 5.17 for a blackline master for the strategy.)	Completion of Reader's Questions assignment
Extend the Learner	Suggested time: 20–25 minutes	Reflective Lesson Log (See Chapter 6, Figure 6.15, for an illustration and Figure 6.28 for a blackline master for the strategy.)	Completion of Reflective Lesson Log

Figure 7.11

SOME PARTING THOUGHTS

In conclusion, this text has presented a myriad of strategies and activities that teachers can utilize as they teach in a block schedule. While I realize that the strategies suggested for each phase and incorporated in the lesson plan examples presented above are often used in traditional 45- to 50-minute class periods, I hope that as you use them in your block schedule classroom, you will realize their real power, for when they are utilized in an extended time frame, students are allocated additional time to complete the strategies and activities in-depth and with greater understanding, thereby not only intensifying the learning experience for them but assuring that their learning is successful.

The lesson plan format presented in this book and the strategies and activities embedded in it have been shared with a number of both novice and experienced teachers at the middle and high school levels. The following comments, representative of the many others uttered again and again by teachers I have worked with, give testimony to the success they and their students have achieved by using the strategies detailed in this text:

- The strategies I learned for use during the block schedule really helped my students think and process.
- My students really enjoyed the creative element that so many of the strategies encompass. I could tell their learning improved because of the types of questions they asked, the answers they gave, and the improved scores on their quizzes and tests.
- It was amazing to see that the strategies I used actually generated class discussions among the students. To accomplish this with special education students is often a difficult task, but the strategies made it easy for them to become engaged and stay engaged.
- Using the learning strategies during the various phases of my block was a huge success for my students. Proceeding through the phases of the lesson was synergistic, and my students read the assigned materials with an in-depth intent. When I took a survey of which method the students preferred—traditional lecture, discussion, and worksheets versus these newfangled strategies—they voted 100% for the newfangled strategies. I am embarrassed to have been so ineffective for so long!
- Again and again, as I used the strategies in my block scheduled class, I realized that they definitely required students to use higher order thinking skills.

I hope you find the lesson plan format and the strategies and activities detailed in this text equally successful.

CHAPTER SUMMARY

This final chapter summarizes the four-pronged lesson plan format designed for use during the 90-minute block scheduled classroom and lists the strategies and activities that are appropriate for use in each phase of it. In addition, ideas are provided for how these strategies and activities can be utilized across the content area disciplines of English, language arts, science, social studies, mathematics, health, family and consumer science, business and technology, foreign language, and fine arts.

References

ABC News. (1993, January 23). Common miracles—the new revolution in American learning [Television broadcast]. New York: American Broadcasting Corporation.

Adams, C. (n.d.). Guidelines for Participants in a Socratic Seminar. Retrieved November 6, 2008, from http://www.studyguide.org/socratic_seminar .htm#Guidelines

Alfassi, M. (1998). Reading for meaning: The efficacy of reciprocal teaching in fostering reading comprehension in high school students in remedial reading classes. *American Educational Research Journal, 35*(2), 309–332.

Alvermann, D. E. (1991). The discussion web: A graphic aid for learning across the curriculum. *The Reading Teacher, 45*(2), 92–99.

Alvermann, D. E., & Phelps, S. F. (2001). *Content reading and literacy: Succeeding in today's diverse classrooms.* Boston: Allyn & Bacon.

Anderson, L. W., & Krathwohl, D. R. (Eds.). (2001). *A taxonomy for learning, teaching, and assessing: A revision of Bloom's Taxonomy of educational objectives.* New York: Addison Wesley Longman.

Armbruster, B., Anderson, T., Armstrong, J., Wise, M., Janisch, C., & Meyer, L. (1991). Reading and questioning in content areas. *Journal of Reading Behavior, 23*(1), 35–59.

Aronson, E., Stephan, C., Sikes, J., Blaney, N., & Snapp, M. (1978). *The jigsaw classroom.* Beverly Hills: Sage.

At the Turning Point: The Young Adolescent Learner (n.d.). Retrieved November 2, 2008, from http://www.turningpts.org/pdf/YALGuide2.pdf

Atwell, N. (1987). *In the middle: Writing, reading, and learning with adolescents.* Portsmouth, NH: Heinemann.

Baker, L., & Brown, A. L. (1984). Metacognitive skills and reading. In P. D. Pearson (Ed.), *Handbook of reading research* (Vol. I, pp. 353–394). New York: Longman.

Ball, W. H. (1996). Socratic Questioning: Then and now. In R. L. Canady & M. Rettig, *Teaching in the block: Strategies for engaging active learners* (pp. 29–64). Cranbury, NJ: Eye on Education.

Beck, I. L., McKeown, M. G., Hamilton, R. L., & Kucan, L. (1997). *Questioning the author: An approach to enhancing student engagement with text.* Newark, DE: International Reading Association.

Bellanca, J., & Fogarty, R. (2003). *Blueprints for achievement in the cooperative classroom.* Glenview, IL: Pearson Professional Development.

Blachowicz, C. L. Z. (1991). Vocabulary instruction in content classes for special needs learners: Why and how? *Journal of Reading, Writing, and Learning Disabilities International, 7*(4), 297–308.

Bransford, J., Brown, A., & Cocking, R. (2000). *How people learn: Brain, mind, experience, and school.* Washington, DC: National Academy Press.

Buehl, D. (2001). *Classroom strategies for interactive learning.* Newark, DE: International Reading Association.

Bugaj, S. J. (1999). Teacher/administrator perceptions of intensive scheduling: Implications for secondary gifted students. *NASSP Bulletin, 83*(610), 62–69.

Burke, K. (2005). *How to assess authentic learning* (4th ed.). Thousand Oaks, CA: Corwin.

Busching, B. A., & Slesinger, B. A. (1995). Authentic questions: What do they look like? Where do they lead? *Language Arts, 72*(5), 341–351.

Caine, R., & Caine, G. (2008). *Overview of the systems principles of natural learning.* Retrieved July 15, 2008, from http://www.cainelearning.com/files/Principles_ overview.pdf

Calkins, L. (1994). *The art of teaching writing.* Portsmouth, NH: Heinemann.

Canady, R. L., & Rettig, M. (1995). *Block scheduling: A catalyst for change in high schools.* Cranbury, NJ: Eye on Education.

Canady, R. L., & Rettig, M. (1996). Block scheduling: What is it? Why do it? How do we harness its potential to improve teaching and learning? In R. L. Canady & M. Rettig, *Teaching in the block: Strategies for engaging active learners* (pp. 1–28). Cranbury, NJ: Eye on Education.

Carter, C. J. (1997). Why reciprocal teaching? *Educational Leadership, 54*(6), 64–68.

Cazden, C. B. (2001). *Classroom discourse: The language of teaching and learning.* Portsmouth, NH: Heinemann.

Center for Teaching Excellence. (2007a). *Level and types of questions.* Retrieved March 10, 2007, from http://www.oir.uiuc.edu/Did/docs/QUESTION/ quest1.htm

Center for Teaching Excellence. (2007b). *Planning questions.* Retrieved March 10, 2007, from http://www.oir.uiuc.edu/Did/docs/QUESTION/quest2.htm

Ciardello, A. V. (1998). You ask a good question today? Alternative cognitive and metacognitive strategies. *Journal of Adolescent and Adult Literacy, 42*(3), 210–219.

Cioffi, G. (1992). Perspective and experience: Developing critical reading abilities. *Journal of Reading, 36*(6), 48–53.

Commander, N. E., & Smith, B. D. (1996). Learning logs: A tool for cognitive monitoring. *Journal of Reading, 39*(6), 446–453.

Cowen, G., & Cowen, E. (1980). *Writing.* New York: Wiley.

Crapse, L. (1995). Helping students construct meaning through their own questions. *Journal of Reading, 38*(5), 389–390.

Crawford, G. B. (2007). *Brain-based teaching with adolescent learning in mind.* Thousand Oaks, CA: Corwin.

Cross, K., & Angelo, T. (1988). Classroom assessment techniques: A handbook for faculty. Ann Arbor, MI: National Center for Research to Improve Postsecondary Teaching and Learning.

Csikszentmihalyi, M. (1990). *Flow: The psychology of optimal experience.* New York: Harper & Row.

deBono, E. (1992). *Serious creativity.* New York: Harper Collins.

Dillion, J. T. (2004). *Questioning and teaching: A manual of practice.* New York: Resource.

Duffelmeyer, F. A., Baum, D. D., & Merkley, D. J. (1987). Maximizing reader-text confrontation with an extended anticipation guide. *Journal of Reading, 31*(2), 146–150.

Durkin, D. (1979). What classroom observations reveal about reading comprehension. *Reading Research Quarterly, 14*(4), 481–533.

Elbow, P. (1973). *Writing without teachers.* London: Oxford University Press.

Ellis, E. (2004). *About graphic organizers: Q & A: What's the big deal with graphic organizers.* Northport, AL: Makes Sense Publishing. Retrieved November 17, 2008, from http://graphicorganizers.com/about.html

Fisher, D., & Frey, D. (2008). *Improving adolescent literacy: Content area strategies at work.* Upper Saddle River, NJ: Pearson Education.

Fogarty, R. (2002). *Brain-compatible classrooms* (2nd ed.). Thousand Oaks, CA: Corwin.

Fogarty, R., Perkins, D., & Barell. (1992). *How to teach for transfer (The mindful school).* Palatine, IL: IRI/SkyLight Training and Publishing.

Gall, M. D. (1984). Synthesis of research on teachers' questioning. *Educational Leadership, 42*(3), 40–47.

Gardner, H. (1983). *Frames of mind.* New York: Basic Books.

Gere, A. (Ed.). (1985). *Roots in the sawdust: Writing to learn across disciplines.* Urbana, IL: National Council of Teachers of English.

Goodlad, J. (1984). *A place called school: Prospects for the future.* New York: McGraw-Hill.

Gopnik, A., Meltzoff, A., & Kuhl, P. (1999). *The scientist in the crib: Minds, brains, and how children learn.* New York: Norton.

Gottfried, A. E., Fleming, J. S., & Gottfried, A. W. (2001). Continuity of academic intrinsic motivation from childhood through later adolescence: A longitudinal study. *Journal of Educational Psychology, 93*(1), 3–13.

Guszak, F. J. (1967). Teacher questioning and reading. *The Reading Teacher, 21*(3), 227–234.

Harste, J. C., Short, K., & Burke, C. L. (1988). *Creating classrooms for authors.* Portsmouth, NH: Heinemann.

Harste, J. C., Woodward, V. A., & Burke, C. L. (1984). *Language stories and literary lessons.* Portsmouth, NH: Heinemann.

Herber, H. (1978). *Teaching reading in content areas* (2nd ed.). Englewood Cliffs, NJ: Prentice Hall.

Heward, W. L. (1994). Three low-tech strategies for increasing the frequency of active student response during group instruction. In R. Gardner III, D. M. Sainato, J. O. Cooper, T. E. Heron, W. L. Heward, J. W. Eshleman, et al. (Eds.), *Behavior analysis in education: Focus on measurably superior instruction* (pp. 285–320). Pacific Grove, CA: Brooks/Cole.

Irvin, J. L., Buehl, D. R., & Radcliffe, B. J. (2007). *Strategies to enhance literacy and learning in the middle school classroom.* Boston: Pearson Education.

Jacobs, H. H. (1997). *Mapping the big picture: Integrating curriculum and assessment, K–12.* Alexandria, VA: Association for Supervision and Curriculum Development.

Jacobs, H. H. (2004). *Getting results with curriculum mapping.* Alexandria, VA: Association for Supervision and Curriculum Development.

Johnson, D. W., & Johnson, R. (1979). Conflict in the classroom: Controversy and learning. *Review of Educational Research, 49*(1), 51–69.

Johnson, D. W., & Johnson, R. (1999). *Methods of cooperative learning: What can we prove works?* Edina, MN: Cooperative Learning Institute.

Johnson, D. W., Johnson, R., & Holubec, E. J. (1993). *Circles of learning: Cooperation in the classroom.* Edina, MN: Interaction Book.

Johnston, P. (1985). Writing to learn in science. In R. A. Gere (Ed.), *Roots in the sawdust: Writing to learn across disciplines* (pp. 92–103). Urbana, IL: National Council of Teachers of English.

Joyce, B. R., Weil, M., & Calhoun, E. (2003). *Models of teaching.* Englewood Cliffs, NJ: Prentice Hall.

Kagan, M., Robertson, L., & Kagan, S. (1995). Cooperative learning structures for classbuilding, San Clemente, CA: Kagan Cooperative Learning.

Kagan, S. (1994). *Cooperative learning.* San Juan Capistrano, CA: Resources for Teachers.

Kamil, M. L. (2003) *Adolescents and literacy: Reading for the 21st century.* Washington, DC: Alliance for Excellent Education.

Keene, E., & Zimmerman, S. (1997). *Mosaic of thought.* Portsmouth, NH: Heinemann.

Knight, J. (2005). *Instructional coaching: A partnership approach to improving instruction.* Thousand Oaks, CA: Corwin.

Lambert, N. M., & McCombs, B. L. (1998). Introduction: Learner-centered schools and classrooms as a direction for school reform. In N. M. Lambert & B. L. McCombs (Eds.), *How students learn* (pp. 1–22). Washington, DC: American Psychological Association.

Langer, J. A. (2001). Beating the odds: Teaching middle and high school students to read and write well. *American Educational Research Journal, 38*(4), 837–880.

Linn, R., Baker, E., & Dunbar, S. (1991). Complex performance-based assessment: Expectations and validation criteria. *Educational Researcher, 20*(8), 15–21.

Lyman, F. T. (1981). The responsive classroom discussion: The inclusion of all students. In A. Anderson (Ed.), *Mainstreaming digest* (pp. 109–113). College Park: University of Maryland Press.

Manzo, A. V. (1969). The ReQuest procedure. *Journal of Reading, 12*(3), 123–126.

Marzano, R. J., Pickering, D. J., & Pollack, J. E. (2001). *Classroom instruction that works.* Alexandria, VA: Association for Supervision and Curriculum Development.

McGinley, W. J., & Denner, P. R. (1987). Story impressions: A pre-reading/writing activity. *Journal of Reading, 31*(3), 248–253.

McKenna, M. C., Kear, D. J., & Ellsworth, R. A. (1995). Children's attitude toward reading: A national survey. *Reading Research Quarterly, 30*(4), 934–956.

Mehan, H. (1979). *Learning lessons.* Cambridge, MA: Harvard University Press.

Merenbloom, E. Y., & Kalina, B. A. (2007). *Making creative schedules work in middle and high schools.* Thousand Oaks, CA: Corwin

Middendorf, J., & Kalish, A. (1996). The change-up in lectures [Electronic version]. *TRC Newsletter, 8*(1). Retrieved November 18, 2008, from http://www.indiana.edu/~teaching/allabout/pubs/changeups.shtml

Moore, D. W., Alvermann, D. E., & Hinchman, K. A. (2000). *Struggling adolescent readers: A collection of teaching strategies.* Newark DE: International Reading Association.

Moore, D. W., Bean, T. W., Birdyshaw, D., & Rycik, J. A. (1999). Adolescent literacy: A position statement. *Journal of Adolescent and Adult Literacy, 43*(1), 97–111.

Moore, D. W., & Moore, S. A. (1992). Possible sentences. An update. In E. K. Dishner, T. W. Bean, J. E. Readence, & D. W. Moore (Eds.), *Reading in the content areas: Improving classroom instruction* (3rd ed., pp. 196–202). Dubuque, IA: Kendall/Hunt.

Morgan, R. F., Meeks, W., Schollaert, A., & Paul, J. (1986). *Critical reading/thinking skills for the college student.* Dubuque, IA: Kendall Hunt.

Moye, V. H. (1997). *Conditions that support transfer for change.* Arlington Heights, IL: IRI/SkyLight Training and Publishing.

National Association of Secondary School Principals. (2006). *Breaking ranks in the middle.* Reston, VA: Author.

National Commission on Excellence in Education. (1983). *A nation at risk: The imperative for educational reform.* Washington, DC: U.S. Department of Education.

National Reading Panel. (2000). *Teaching children to read: An evidence-based assessment of the scientific research literature on reading and its implications for reading instruction* (NIH Pub. No. 00–4769). Washington, DC: National Institute of Child Health and Human Development.

Oakes, J., & Lipton, M. (1999). *Teaching to change the world.* New York: McGraw-Hill College.

Oldfather, P., & Dahl, K. (1994). Toward a social constructivist reconceptualization of intrinsic motivation for literacy learning. *Journal of Reading Behavior, 26*(2), 139–158.

Otis, N., Grouzer, F., & Pelletier, L. G. (2005). Latent motivational change in an academic setting: A 3-year longitudinal study. *Journal of Educational Psychology, 97*(2), 170–183.

Palincsar, A. S., & Brown, A. L. (1986). Interactive teaching to promote independent learning from text. *The Reading Teacher, 39*(8), 771–777.

Palincsar, A. S., & Herrenkohl, I. R. (2002). Designing collaborative learning contexts. *Theory Into Practice, 41*(1), 26–32.

Paris, S. G., Lipson, M. Y., & Wixson, K. K. (1983). Becoming a strategic reader. *Contemporary Educational Psychology, 8*(3), 293–316.

Paris, S. G., Wasik, B., & Turner, M. (1991). The development of strategic readers. In R. Barr, M. Kamil, P. Mosenthal, & P. D. Pearson (Eds.), *Handbook of Reading Research* (Vol. II, pp. 609–640). New York: Longman.

Pearson, P. D., & Gallagher, M. C. (1983). The instruction of reading comprehension. *Contemporary Educational Psychology, 8*(8), 317–344.

Perkins, D. N. (1992). *Smart minds: From training memories to educating minds.* New York: The Free Press.

Peterson, C. L., Caverly, D. C., Nicholson, S. A., O'Neal, S., & Cusenbary, S. (2000). *Building reading proficiencies at the secondary level: A guide to resources.* Austin: Southwest Texas State University.

Pichert, J. W., & Anderson, R. C. (1977). Taking different perspectives on a story. *Journal of Educational Psychology, 69*(4), 309–315.

Pisapia, J., & Westfall, A. (1997). *Alternative high school schedules: A view from the teacher's desk.* Research report. Richmond, VA: Metropolitan Educational Research Consortium.

Queen, J. A. (2000). Block scheduling revisited. *Phi Delta Kappan, 82*(3), 214–222.

Raphael, T. E., Au, K. H., & Highfield, K. (2006). *QAR now.* New York: Scholastic.

Readence, J. E., Bean, T. W., & Baldwin, R. S. (2004). *Content area literacy: An integrated approach.* Dubuque, IA: Kendall/Hunt.

Richardson, J. S., & Morgan, R. F. (2003). *Reading to learn in the content areas.* Belmont, CA: Wadsworth.

Richgels, D. J., McGee, L. M., Lomas, R. G., & Sheard, C. (1987). Awareness of four text structures: Effects on recall of expository text. *Reading Research Quarterly, 22*(2), 177–196.

Robinson, H. A. (1978, May). *Facilitating successful reading strategies.* Paper presented at International Reading Association Convention, Houston, TX.

Rodrigues, R. J. (1983). Tools for developing prewriting skills. *English Journal, 72*(2), 58–60.

Roe, B. D., Stoodt-Hill, B. D., & Burns, P. C. (2007). *Secondary school literacy instruction: The content areas.* Boston, MA: Houghton Mifflin.

Royer, J. M., Cisero, C. A., & Carlo, N. S. (1993). Techniques and procedures for assessing cognitive skills. *Review of Educational Research, 63*(2), 201–243.

Ryan, R. M., & Deci, E. I. (2000). Self-determination theory and the facilitation of intrinsic motivation, social development, and well-being. *American Psychologist, 55*(1), 68–78.

Santa, C. (1988). *Content reading including study systems.* Dubuque, IA: Kendall/Hunt.

Savion, L., & Middendorf, J. (1994). Enhancing concept comprehension and retention. *National teaching and learning forum, 3*(4), 6–8.

Sejnost, R. L., & Thiese, S. (2007). *Reading and writing across content areas.* Thousand Oaks, CA: Corwin.

Sharan, Y., & Sharan, S. (1992). *Group investigation: A strategy for expanding cooperative learning.* New York: Teachers College Press.

Silberman, M. (1996). *Active learning: 101 strategies to teach any subject.* Boston: Allyn & Bacon.

Silver, H. F., Strong, R. W., & Perini, M. J. (2001). *Tools for promoting active, in-depth learning.* Woodbridge, NJ: Thoughtful Education Press.

Simpson, M. L. (1986). PORPE: A writing strategy for studying ad learning in the content areas. *Journal of Reading, 29*(5), 410–414.

Sizer, T. R. (1996). *Horace's hope: What works for the American high school.* Boston: Houghton Mifflin.

Slavin, R. E. (1994). *Using student team learning* (4th ed.). Baltimore, MD: Johns Hopkins University, Center for Social Organization of Schools.

Smith, P., & Tompkins, G. (1988). Structured notetaking: A new strategy for content areas. *Journal of Reading, 32*(1), 46–53.

Solon, C. (1980). The pyramid diagram: A college study skills tool. *Journal of Reading, 23,* 594–597.

Sousa, D. (2006). *How the brain learns* (3rd ed.). Thousand Oaks, CA: Corwin.

Sturtevant, E. (1992). Content literacy in high school social studies. Two case studies in a multicultural setting. Unpublished dissertation, Kent State University, Kent, Ohio.

Sturtevant, E. G., & Linek, W. M. (2004). *Content literacy: An inquiry-based case study approach.* Upper Saddle River, NJ: Pearson Education.

Sylwester, R. (1995). *A celebration of neurons: An educator's guide to the human brain.* Alexandria, VA: Association for Supervision and Curriculum Development.

Taylor, B. M. (1980). Children's memory for expository text after reading. *Reading Research Quarterly, 15*(3), 399–411.

Tompkins, G. E. (2002). *Language arts: Content and teaching strategies* (5th ed.). Upper Saddle River, NJ: Merrill/Prentice Hall.

Tompkins, G. E. (2004). *50 literacy strategies: Step by step.* Upper Saddle River, NJ: Pearson Education.

Unrau, N. J., & Schlackman, J. (2006). Motivation and its relationship with reading achievement in an urban middle school. *Journal of Educational Research, 100*(1), 81–101.

Vacca, R. T. (2002). From efficient decoders to strategic readers. *Educational Leadership, 60*(3), 7–11.

Vacca, R. T., & Vacca, J. L. (2008). *Content area reading: Literacy and learning across the curriculum.* Boston: Pearson Education.

Van den Broek, P., & Kremer, K. (2000). The mind in action: What it means to comprehend during reading. In B. M. Taylor, M. Graves, & P. Van den Broek (Eds.), *Reading for meaning: Fostering comprehension in the middle grades* (pp. 1–31). New York: Teachers College Press.

Vaughan, C. L. (1990). Knitting writing: The double-entry journal. In N. Atwell (Ed.), *Coming to know: Writing to learn in the intermediate grades* (pp. 69–75). Portsmouth: Heinemann.

Vaughan, J., & Estes, T. (1986). *Reading and reasoning beyond the primary grades.* Boston: Allyn & Bacon.

Walsh, J. A., & Sattes, B. D. (2005). *Questioning and understanding to improve learning and thinking: Teacher manual* (2nd ed.). Charleston, WV: Appalachia Educational Laboratory.

Weaver, R. L., & Cotrell, H. W. (1985). Mental aerobics: The half-sheet response. *Innovative Higher Education, 10*(1), 23–31.

Whitehead, D. (1994). Teaching literacy and learning strategies through a modified guided silent reading procedure. *Journal of Reading, 38*(1), 24–30.

Whiteley, S. (2005). *Memletics concept mapping course.* Des Plaines, IL: Advanogy.

Williams, R. B., & Dunn, S. E. (2008). *Brain-compatible learning for the block* (2nd ed.). Thousand Oaks, CA: Corwin.

Willis, J. (2007). Brain-based teaching strategies for improving students' memory, learning, and test-taking success. *Childhood Education, 83*(5), 310–315.

Wilson, R. C. (1986). Improving faculty teaching: Effective use of the student evaluations and consultants. *Journal of Higher Education, 57*(2), 196–211.

Wimer, J. W., Ridenour, C. S., & Thomas, K. (2001). Higher order teacher questioning of boys and girls in elementary mathematics classrooms. *Journal of Educational Research, 95*(2), 84–92.

Winograd, P., & Hare, V. C. (1988). Direct instruction of reading comprehension strategies: The nature of teacher explanation. In C. E. Weinstein, E. T. Goetz, &

P. A. Alexander (Eds.), *Learning and study strategies: Issues in assessment, instruction, and evaluation* (pp. 121–139). San Diego, CA: Academic Press.

Wolfe, P. (2001). *Brain matters: Translating research into classroom practice.* Alexandria, VA: Association for Supervision and Curriculum Development.

Wood, K. D. (1996). Evaluation and testing: The road less traveled. In S. J. Silverman & C. D. Ennis (Eds.), *Student learning in physical education* (pp. 100–219). Champaign, IL: Human Kinetics.

Young, T. A., & Daines, D. (1992). Student's predictive questions and their teachers' pre-questions about expository text in grades K–5. *Reading Psychology, 13*(4), 291–308.

Zemelman, S., & Daniels, H. (1988). *A community of writers.* Portsmouth, NH: Heinemann.

Index

The Corwin logo—a raven striding across an open book—represents the union of courage and learning. Corwin is committed to improving education for all learners by publishing books and other professional development resources for those serving the field of PreK–12 education. By providing practical, hands-on materials, Corwin continues to carry out the promise of its motto: **"Helping Educators Do Their Work Better."**